HIGH
OCTANE
WOMEN

MORE PRAISE FOR *HIGH-OCTANE WOMEN*

"Dr. Carter's book is the perfect and much-needed fuel to recharge my 'high-octane' engine."

—Stacy M. Ross
Criminal court judge and active community volunteer

"Wow! A complete and life-transforming journey of enlightenment, recognition, solutions, and relief! As an entrepreneur working alone in a home office, I was surprised to learn that I am a high-octane woman. I found answers to questions I've had for many years and now feel supported and validated. Dr. Bourg Carter's book is a must-read for all women working in or outside the home and is a great support tool for their families as well. I like to highlight the best parts of a book to review later, but *High-Octane Women* was becoming completely covered in yellow highlights! The research and preparation for this book is evident and appreciated. Thank you, thank you, THANK YOU!"

—Kelly Rudolph
Author, speaker, personal safety trainer, positive woman coach
KellyRudolph.com

HIGH OCTANE WOMEN

How Superachievers Can Avoid
BURNOUT

Dr. Sherrie Bourg Carter

Prometheus Books

59 John Glenn Drive
Amherst, New York 14228-2119

Published 2011 by Prometheus Books

Cover design by Jacqueline Nasso Cooke
Cover image © Media Bakery

Inquiries should be addressed to
Prometheus Books
59 John Glenn Drive
Amherst, New York 14228–2119
VOICE: 716–691–0133
FAX: 716–691–0137
WWW.PROMETHEUSBOOKS.COM

14 13 12 11 10   5 4 3 2 1

Library of Congress Cataloging-in-Publication Data

Bourg Carter, Sherrie.
    High-octane women : how superachievers can avoid burnout / Sherrie Bourg Carter.
        p. cm.
    Includes bibliographical references and index.
    ISBN 978–1–61614–220–9 (pbk.)
    1. Burn out (Psychology) 2. Job stress. 3. Women executives—Health and hygiene.
4. Stress management for women. I. Title.

BF481.B685 2010
158.7'23082—dc22

2010029633

Printed in the United States of America

For Jennifer and Jessie

CONTENTS

ACKNOWLEDGMENTS

Writing a book is a challenging journey, much of which is spent alone with a computer. But on this journey, I was fortunate enough to have an amazing pit crew that worked hard behind the scenes to get me across the finish line.

To my agent, Grace Freedson, who believed in this project from the beginning and provided sound guidance throughout the process.

To my editor at Prometheus Books, Linda Regan, whose professionalism, insightfulness, availability, and candor were invaluable to me as we maneuvered our way through the editing process.

To my partner, Dr. Michael Brannon, whose support and hard work have provided me with the time and the opportunity to write this book.

To my friend Renee Haubner, who took time out of her own high-achieving life to read countless pages of manuscript and provide loving doses of support and encouragement throughout the journey.

To my family, who supported me every step of the way.

To my high-octane daughters, who unselfishly gave up "our" time so that I could have enough "me" time to write this book.

And to all the high-octane women I have had the distinct privilege of knowing, without whom this book could not have been written.

You are the best team I could have ever asked for, and for that, you have my deepest respect and gratitude.

AUTHOR'S NOTES

Throughout this book, the names and identifying details of women I have befriended, interviewed, or counseled over the past twenty-five years have been changed to protect their identities, and most of the persons described are a composite of several women with similar life experiences.

The advice offered in this book should be viewed as general recommendations for understanding and reducing stress to promote a healthier, happier, and more productive lifestyle and to avoid burnout. It is not intended to be a substitute for the type of individualized treatment planning and recommendations that can be offered only by private psychological counseling or psychiatric care. If readers are experiencing any troubling symptoms similar to those described in this book, it is recommended that they consult with a mental health professional. The advice offered in this book should not be used as a substitute for personalized professional care.

INTRODUCTION

THE RISE AND FALL OF ATHENA

Athena and I met in graduate school. She was one of those superstar law students: full scholarship, law journal editor, couldn't make a B if she tried. You know the type. I was a psychology major studying forensics, which brought me to the law school once or twice a week. It was Athena's interest in mental health law that brought us together and led to a friendship that endured well beyond our school days.

After we graduated, our careers pretty much took over our lives. Within Athena's first year out of school, her law practice was thriving, as anyone who knew her expected it would. My psychology practice was busy as well, so we didn't see each other as often as we would have liked. And, of course, on top of our crazy work schedules, we had our families and other relationships to attend to, as well as a host of other responsibilities and commitments, all of which made it hard to find time to breathe, much less eat or socialize. Still, we did our best to get together for lunch once a month to catch up.

We had scheduled a lunch date in December to share some holiday cheer, but the frenetic pace of the season forced us to cancel. We rescheduled for January, but one of her "catastrophes of constitutional proportions," as she liked to say, caused that to get scratched as well. And so it went, on and on, for the next few months, until July arrived.

It was a sweltering South Florida day. The heat index was forecast to top 100 degrees, and I was dressed in a suit for court later that day, which made the prospect of going outside at lunchtime not particularly inviting. The growing piles of work on my desk weren't helping my motivation either. But something inside me, something in Athena's voice when we had set up the lunch told me I shouldn't cancel this one, and I'm glad I didn't.

When I pulled up to the restaurant and saw her walking across the parking lot, I could tell something was wrong. Athena was seated by the time I got inside, and when I walked up to the table, her halfhearted smile confirmed my suspicion.

"Bad day?" I asked as soon as I sat down. After ten years of friendship, you get a pass on preliminary pleasantries.

13

"If it was only a day," she responded with that same halfhearted smile.

"What happened?" I asked, only later realizing how naive the question was.

She dropped her head and hesitated before responding. "The funny thing is," she said, "I'm not sure exactly what happened. I couldn't even tell you when it happened. All I know is that at some point, my life went from everything I ever wanted to everything I never wanted."

The restaurant was noisy with a bustling lunch crowd, and I thought—or rather hoped—that I hadn't heard her correctly. My friend, the woman who had defied the odds and valiantly climbed to the peak of one of the most patriarchal mountains in the world, the woman who could perform amazing feats with seemingly no effort, wasn't talking about a bad day or a bad ruling or a bad verdict. I had seen those "bad days" and this wasn't one of them. This was something much bigger.

"I keep thinking if I could just go back in time," she continued, "and find the point when it all changed, I could change it back. But I can't seem to focus long enough to go back that far. All I know is that I don't want to do this anymore. I feel like all I am is my work. But I'm afraid if I stop, I'll no longer exist. Does that make any sense?" She looked down, feigning interest in the menu.

Whoa! I sat there stunned, not believing what I was hearing. This was so far beyond a bad day. I knew I should say something profound yet comforting. After all, I was the psychologist. But what do you say when someone who by all objective measures seems to "have it all" suddenly tells you she doesn't want it anymore?

A rush of thoughts and feelings raced through my head. I managed to recover enough to eke out a few lame words of encouragement—"But you love what you do," "No one else could fill your shoes," "This will pass"—the same kind of comments I have since heard so many others say when their own superstars seemed to be falling from the sky. But when lunch ended and we returned to our respective hectic lives, I had a feeling that the Athena I knew would not be coming back.

That was ten years ago. It's easy now to look back on that experience with some perspective and, of course, ten more years of experience—ten years of talking to other high-achieving women about their lives, their successes, and their challenges. I learned a lot of lessons during that time, but one of the most important was that I was wrong about a lot of things on that day in July.

I was wrong in thinking that I understood what Athena was talking about when she asked if she was making any sense. The truth is, I was seeing only the tip of a very large and very dangerous iceberg. And, unfortunately, it's an iceberg that continues to grow in a corporate world that fails to see the need for change in the face of a changed society, a society very different from what it was just a few decades ago. I was also wrong in believing (and hoping) that if Athena would have just given her job a little more time, everything would have worked out.

But there was one thing I was right about: Athena was not coming back. The day after that lunch, she called to tell me that she had quit her job.

Athena's engine had burned out.

HIGH-ACHIEVING WOMEN AND BURNOUT

Although I didn't know it at the time, Athena's unexpected and untimely exit from the work world planted the seeds for what would ultimately become this book, *High-Octane Women: How Superachievers Can Avoid Burnout*. My conversations with Athena about her reasons for leaving her job prompted countless other conversations over the years with other high-achieving women, who, like Athena, once had boundless energy, big dreams, and enormous enthusiasm; women who at one time were all racing along at two hundred miles per hour with their sights set squarely on the next finish line, feeling all the joy and excitement that come with success. And just like Athena, the possibility of burnout never entered their minds . . . until it happened.

These women were the best and the brightest the world had to offer: doctors, lawyers, CEOs, community leaders, professors. They worked hard, but they loved their jobs and the challenges that came along with them. They loved the excitement. They loved the adrenaline rush. They loved working with others who were equally gifted. They were intelligent problem solvers who loved fixing things that were broken. They weren't naive or ignorant of the dangers of stress. They understood it. They recognized its consequences. The problem was that they didn't recognize the true extent—the enormity—of what they were up against until it was too late.

Burnout with a Twist

Burnout isn't a new concept. It's been studied for decades, beginning in the 1970s by pioneers like clinical psychologist Herbert Freudenberger and social psychologist Christina Maslach, both of whom came across the syndrome in their studies of human service workers. Although the definition has been refined over the years as new research has emerged, the central aspect of burnout has generally centered around job-related interpersonal stress and its psychological toll on workers.[1] But what I was seeing and hearing from high-achieving women was more than job-related stress. Much more. I discovered that high-achieving women add a new twist to the concept of burnout, a twist that unfortunately makes them even more vulnerable to it.

The first step in understanding burnout in high-achieving women lies in understanding its insidious nature. Unlike a blowout, which is instant and obvious, burnout is a slow leak, a cumulative process that in most instances takes years, sometimes decades to fully materialize. By definition, burnout occurs when chronic stress and frustration lead to:

- physical and emotional exhaustion,
- feelings of cynicism and detachment, and
- a sense of ineffectiveness and lack of accomplishment.[2]

Once burnout overtakes its victim, it is difficult to overcome, even for a normal worker with normal job-related stress. But high-achieving women are not normal workers with normal job-related stress. They're *extraordinary* women with *extraordinary life-related* stressors—unique and multidimensional stressors that make them particularly vulnerable to experiencing burnout.

Today's high-achieving women are bombarded with stress from every conceivable direction. The most publicized (and therefore the most recognized) type of stress is that caused by work—high-pressure jobs, long hours, and heavy workloads. But for high-achieving women, it doesn't stop there. Despite the overall gains made toward gender equality in the last few decades, the unfortunate truth is that double binds, double standards, gender discrimination, and gender stereotypes continue to play a significant role in the stress women experience in the workplace.

In fact, a recent article in the *American Bar Association Journal* illustrates that double standards and gender discrimination are very much alive and well in the twenty-first century. The article cites an e-mail sent by a partner in a UK law firm, a firm that ironically was praised for its commitment to equality and diversity. The e-mail, sent to a department head about a job applicant who had recently given birth, asked, "Are there any guidelines on how we can ask questions properly designed to identify her commitment, hours she is prepared to do, how she will balance work and a child?" A former partner who resigned from the firm shortly after the e-mail was leaked said that such inquiries were not made for male job applicants and aptly noted that such an e-mail would likely compromise the woman's prospects for employment.[3]

Another example comes from Jackie, a defense lawyer and mother of two: "I had a trial scheduled on the same day that my preschooler was appearing in a play at her school. I knew about the conflict well in advance, so I set a hearing a month before to ask that the trial date be reset. The judge gave me a new date, but he not-so-jokingly told me that maybe I should 'reevaluate my career choice' if my child's life was going to interfere in my ability to do my job. When men ask for time off to do something with their kids, they're heralded as superdads. I, on the other hand, apparently should have turned in my Bar Card on the way to the hospital to give birth!"

Work-related stress, however, is only part of the stress that high-achieving women experience. As Susan, a business owner and PTA board member, put it, "Please. If it was just my job, there wouldn't be anything to talk about. I can handle the job stress. It's all the other things on top of my job that just peck away at me until by the end of the day, I'm running on reserves."

These "other things" Susan is referring to are stressors that are difficult to quantify because they're so broad. They range from internal to external, societal to familial, personal to interpersonal, biological to technological, and all points in between.

For example, conflicting societal expectations can add considerable stress to the lives of high-achieving women. In fact, many experience the sting of these conflicting expectations in one form or another at some point during their lives. "You're going to go to graduate school, aren't you? You're too bright not to get an advanced degree," followed by "How old are you now? Do you have a boyfriend? Don't you want to get married and raise a family?" or "You leave your child in daycare from seven in the morning until six at night? *Every* day?" followed by a righteous indignant look. Although society may have accepted a woman's right to sit alongside men in academia and the workforce, the expectation that women should study or work as long and as hard as men while also continuing to fulfill all the other "duties" society adds to their plate seems to somehow have left the reality of a twenty-four-hour day out of the equation.

Technology also pushes the limits of a twenty-four-hour day. The unending barrage of beeps and buzzes from gadgets that keep workers on alert 24/7 adds significant stress to already stress-filled lives, particularly for women in high-level positions or those who own their own businesses. In fact, in today's technologically advanced world, it's rare to find someone who isn't "connected" in some way.

But being constantly connected is only part of the problem. The other part is the expectation of a quick response to what often amounts to hundreds of e-mails, instant messages, pages, phone messages, and text messages that come across the multitude of screens most people seem to be glued to nearly all hours of the day and night.

And these are only the external sources of stress! The internal ones, those self-perpetuating internal wars that so many women wage with themselves, can be just as damaging, if not more so. Perfectionism, guilt, over-commitment, reluctance to delegate, and not setting realistic limits are all examples of internally generated stressors common among high achievers. And then there is the never-ending "tick, tick, ticking" of those biological clocks, an issue that most high-achieving women struggle with at some point (often at many points) in their lives. These proverbial clocks, whispering in the backs of their minds, "If you wait too long, you won't be able to [fill in the blank]," along with societal expectations that women should not only be able to do it all, but that they should do it all with a June Cleaver smile on their faces, can create enormous inner turmoil for successful women.

The Costs of Burnout

The stressors I've described can prove extremely costly for high-achieving women—and the toll is not only a financial one. Physically, the costs can include chronic fatigue, loss of appetite or overeating, weight loss or weight gain, headaches, and/or sleep problems. Over time, chronic stress can also lead to heart disease, heart attack, high blood pressure, ulcers, and a variety of other medical conditions. Psychologically, symptoms may include irritability, depression, anger, nightmares, feeling trapped, feeling emotionally depleted, and/or feeling hopeless, helpless, and alone. Abuse of alcohol, drugs, food, and tobacco also are common in cases of burnout, not to mention the enormous interpersonal stress that problems like these often cause: marital distress, divorce, and tension in other relationships, to name only a few. In short, burnout can destroy lives.

But the costs aren't just personal. Businesses suffer as well. When our best and our brightest women burn out, companies not only lose billions of dollars each year as a result of lowered productivity, increased absenteeism, and sick leave, they also lose the enormous talent and opportunities these women create. The truth is that women add unique perspectives to businesses and politics that men do not, perspectives that come from experiencing life as a woman. In fact, studies have found that when smart, ambitious, and dedicated women enter the mix, good things happen—new ideas are generated, the bottom line often improves, and businesses and society benefit.[4] And when someone can offer these kinds of opportunities and benefits—regardless of their gender—it is a valuable commodity that is difficult to replace.

SOLUTIONS

Because you're reading this book, it's likely that you or someone you know is a high-achieving woman looking for solutions, concrete strategies that will reduce what at times probably feels like an insurmountable amount of stress. The reason it feels overwhelming is because, if you're like most high-achieving women, stress is flying at you from every conceivable direction. Just when it seems like you've deflected one blow, several others fly at you from a different direction, making effective solutions seem elusive.

For example, let's say that you've worked very hard to overcome your personal demons, like perfectionism and overcommitting yourself. That's great . . . except there are likely to be hundreds of other stressors in your life that are still there, chipping away at you. If there isn't an effort from all sides to decrease stress, positive change is obviously going to be more difficult to achieve.

In addition, traditional stress-management strategies aren't always particularly helpful to high-achieving women. Why? Because, as I noted before, you're different. Your job choices, lifestyle, habits, and personality are intense. It's this intensity that makes you who you are; it's what makes you thrive and shine in comparison to everyone else. But it also makes it a challenge to find stress-management strategies that don't strip away the essence of who you are.

Traditional relaxation techniques, like massage, warm baths, yoga, meditation, vacations, and guided imagery, are effective in calming most people. But there's a reason you're reading this book and not the volumes of stress-management books flooding the market these days. For decades, high-achieving women have been told by a host of experts on stress management that if they want to achieve y (stress reduction), they need to do x (traditional stress-reduction techniques). But what if x doesn't bring about y for you? Many of the high-achieving women I've worked with over the years have taken this to mean that there is something wrong with them. They have trouble accepting that of all the amazing feats they have been able to accomplish in their lives and careers, the one that seems so simple—reducing stress—seems out of reach.

There is no better example of this than Marilyn, a CFO of a large accounting firm. Marilyn came to me feeling frustrated and defeated. "You're going to tell me to slow down, take a spa vacation, meditate," she said. "But none of that has ever worked for me. I honestly would rather walk across a bed of nails. At least that would engage my brain. I don't know what's wrong with me." The reality is that there was nothing wrong with Marilyn. And there is nothing wrong with you.

Are you normal? No. But you never have been, and the truth is, you've never wanted to be. As a high-achieving woman, you're driven by a different kind of engine. You think differently. You work differently. You stress differently. And, in many cases, you de-stress differently. So if x doesn't work for you, don't beat yourself up over it. It's just not the right kind of fuel for your high-performance engine. And the more pressure you put on yourself to make x work for you, the more stress you bring into your life and the more at risk you are for burnout.

Does this mean you don't need refueling? No. Everyone needs refueling. The key is to find the right fuel for your engine. Once you do that, you can determine the best course to get you back on track, to what you thrive on: the healthy challenges of an active, accomplished, and productive life. That means finding unique solutions that will work for your unique circumstances. And that is the purpose of this book: to offer you a road map that will help you discover the right solutions to reduce stress and avoid burnout in your life.

RESTARTING YOUR ENGINE

One of the first questions I'm asked by high-achieving women who are trying to overcome burnout is: "How long will this take?" It's understandable. High-achieving women are used to finding quick solutions to problems so they can move on to the next one. The difference here, of course, is that burnout isn't your run-of-the-mill problem. It doesn't happen overnight and it's not going to go away overnight. So the honest answer to the question is: It depends on how far along you are on the path to burnout.

But I can tell you this. If you're expecting to just skip to the end and find the "answers," this is not the book for you. There is no seven-day program or twenty-one-step program within these pages. I'm not going to have you take any tests to see if you're a high-achieving woman. If you are, you know it. You don't need a test to tell you. You are unique, and the only "program" that is going to work for you is the one you discover for yourself. My job is to put you on the right path to make that discovery by first helping you become more aware of what you're up against in terms of stress from the workplace, society, technology, and, in many cases, your own way of viewing the world. Then we'll take a look at your current stress level and determine how close you are to burnout. Finally, we'll explore strategies that you can use when plotting your new course to a healthy, happy, and less stressed life.

So, are you ready? Well, then, start your engines.

PART ONE:

ON YOUR MARK

Chapter 1

THE AMAZING RACE:
Women's Achievements and Challenges

The Amazing Race: *CBS reality show in which participants race around the globe to find clues that will lead them to the grand prize.*

—from CBS.com

"You quit?" I repeated in disbelief. "You run an entire litigation department. Are you sure you want to do this?" I fell into my chair, kicking myself for not seeing this coming and wondering if she was making a huge mistake. Her response gave me the answer.

"I don't run an entire department," Athena sighed. "It runs me."

I went into psychologist mode. "I'm just a little worried about you. You sound like you're giving up."

She laughed. "My mom and her mom had it a lot harder than I do, and they didn't give up. I'm certainly not going to. I just got a little off-course and I need to find my way back into the race."

Eventually, Athena did find her way back, but as her story and the stories of the many women who came before her exemplify, the roads high-achieving women travel are not always smooth ones. There are bumps and potholes and flying debris that sometimes get in the way. But despite the rough spots, it has been an amazing race!

Ambitious women have been around since the beginning of human history. However, because of rigid social ideology and expectations that lasted well into the mid–twentieth century, most women didn't have opportunities to rise up and shine as they do today.

During World War II, many job opportunities opened up for women, but when the war ended in 1945, most of these opportunities ended as well.[1] Those who did work outside the home found few openings for anything other than the low-paying jobs traditionally viewed as "women's work," such as nursing, teaching, sewing, and retail sales. If nothing else, however, this period in history offered the world and women themselves a glimpse into the future, a foreshadowing of the versatility, industriousness, and talent women would use one day in their race to overcome a barrage of manmade obstacles and climb to the top in a broad range of fields, such as law, medicine, politics, finance, entertainment, and media.

That "day" certainly did not come quickly or easily. After the war, society and government placed an enormous of amount of pressure on women through intensive ad campaigns to return to their "places" in the home and to support their husbands and raise their children. Images of Doris Day, Debbie Reynolds, and the picture-perfect aproned housewife were heavily promoted to quell female ambition and to keep high-achieving women confined to their homes. But society was changing.

Inspired by the civil rights movement, the women's movement gained momentum in the 1960s. Under pressure from former first lady Eleanor Roosevelt and activist Esther Peterson, President John F. Kennedy established the President's Commission on the Status of Women in 1961. Then, in 1963, author and feminist Betty Friedan published *The Feminine Mystique*, a powerful critique on the subjugation of women, which gave a voice to women dissatisfied with the rigid role restrictions placed upon them by society.[2] That same year, Congress passed the Equal Pay Act, making it illegal for employers to pay women less than men for the same work. In 1964, discrimination based on race and sex was barred by Title VII of the Civil Rights Act. In the 1970s, bans on education discrimination, pregnancy discrimination, and credit discrimination were passed. The end of the century brought even more progress, rallying well-deserved attention to the issues of sexual harassment and violence against women.[3] And although more progress is still needed, women have made amazing strides.

CLOSING THE GAP

Today, there isn't a job anywhere in the world that hasn't been held by a woman. Each day, more and more women are clearing that proverbial glass ceiling and rising to positions that many would not have believed possible only a few decades ago. Although men still dominate many of the most powerful positions in business and politics, women are closing the gap.

Forty years ago, women accounted for only a third of all workers in the United States. Today, for the first time in history, women actually outnumber men in the workforce.[4] More than half of the management and professional positions in the United States are held by women.[5] In addition, female business owners represent one of today's fastest-growing markets, with women making up 35 percent of all self-employed Americans.[6]

Rigid family roles are changing as well. According to a recent *Time* magazine poll, there are now 3.3 million marriages in the United States in which the wife is the sole breadwinner—2.4 million more than in 1970. In the same poll, 40 percent of women reported that they were the primary breadwinners in their households, and 80 percent of those polled, including both men and women, viewed this as positive.[7]

In sports, female athletes are becoming increasingly recognized for their skill and talent. In entertainment, women are topping the charts, with Madonna taking the number-one spot on *Forbes*' list of highest-earning musicians for 2009[8] and Sandra Bullock being touted as 2009's top-earning Hollywood star.[9] In 2010, Kathryn Bigelow became the first woman to win an Oscar for best director.[10] And, in politics, it's hard to ignore the milestones set by women like Secretary of State Hillary Clinton, former governor Sarah Palin, and House Speaker Nancy Pelosi.

These achievements, however, are by no means an indication that all is well on the gender-equality front. Despite enormous advances, women still don't earn equal wages for equal work. At last count, women earned only seventy-seven cents for every dollar earned by men.[11] Although education does play a factor in salary, with higher degrees leading to higher salaries, no matter the degree—doctoral, professional, master's, bachelor's, and associate's—men earn more than women.[12]

Moreover, although women make up half of the workforce, they remain severely underrepresented in higher-paying positions. Fewer than 3 percent of Fortune 500 CEOs are female.[13] Fewer than one-fifth of law firm partners are female.[14] In the engineering field, only 11 percent of jobs are held by women; among physicians, only 30 percent are women; and in math and computer science, just 20 percent of jobs are held by women.[15] These figures are even worse for most minority women, who tend to be paid even less and are seriously underrepresented in the upper echelons of the workforce. And pressing societal issues that impact women the most—limited access to childcare, women's healthcare, and violence against women—remain unresolved.

Yet, if statistics offer a glimpse into our future, the good old boys better start preparing for the good new girls. Seven women were appointed to cabinet-level positions in President Obama's White House, as well as two female Supreme Court justices—Sonia Sotomayor and Elena Kagan. On the political front, we certainly could do better than women holding six gubernatorial positions and 17 percent of congressional seats. But these numbers represent a consistent increase over the last two decades,[16] and they should continue to rise as more and more women become involved in politics and gain experience at state and local levels. In addition, female registered voters outnumber male registered voters by ten million, and in the 2008 presidential election, nearly ten million more women turned out to vote than men.[17]

Education among spouses has also seen a dramatic shift. In 1970, 28 percent of married women had husbands who were better educated than they were. But by 2007, that number reversed, with 28 percent of women being better educated than their husbands.[18] And there is even more promise on the horizon.

In the 1970s, only about 10 percent of law students were female; today the percentage has risen to almost half. The same holds true for the medical profession. And on college campuses, what not too long ago was a 60:40 male-to-female ratio has reversed; now 60 percent of college students are female.[19] Clearly, these and countless other milestones attest to the fact that, more than ever before, women are breaking through gender barriers and rising to unprecedented heights. However, the advancement of women in society and the workplace can cut both ways.

DOUBLE-EDGED SWORD

While high-achieving women are blazing trails to the top of the mountain, little attention is being paid to the perilous terrain that comes with the territory and its negative impact on women's health and well-being. As Dana, a physician in private practice, told me, "If I had known when I entered medical school that my success story would have a prescription for Xanax and Prozac in the footnotes, I'm not sure I'd have taken that road." Unfortunately, she's not alone.

The latest research on women's subjective well-being shows that, by most objective measures, women's life circumstances have improved greatly over the past few decades, but their happiness has declined both absolutely and relative to men.[20] Interestingly, these findings hold true across all categories—among married and divorced women, working mothers and stay-at-home mothers, old and young, and all educational levels. While the answers aren't clear as to exactly why women are less happy, we can no longer afford to ignore the impact of multiple and ever-increasing responsibilities (at home and/or at work) and the stress that accompanies these responsibilities in our lives.

Burnout rates among female workers are on the rise. And living through the worst economic disaster since the Great Depression certainly hasn't improved the situation. In fact, its repercussions are causing tsunamis for countless high-achieving women and their families throughout the world. Financial problems have always been ranked high among life stressors not only because they affect the bottom line but also because they often cause ripple effects that can result in major lifestyle changes, such as relocation, longer work hours, or the need to get a second or third job. In addition, financial problems tend to cause increased conflict and tension in relationships. All these "ripples" can have a profound impact on our stress levels and our health.

For example, I recently received a call from Sheila, a human resources manager at a large marketing firm. She wanted me to speak to her senior-level female employees about coping with stress. When I asked how long a presentation she was looking for, she answered, "How many days do you have available?" I laughed, but she responded, "I'm serious. I feel like I'm practicing psychology without a license these days. It used to be that they would come to me worried about getting a pink slip. Lately, though, it's gone way beyond that—family members moving in because they lost their home, a few are living with husbands they hate because they can't afford a divorce. These are strong women, but even the strongest of the strong have breaking points."

Unfortunately, these are not isolated cases. If statistics tell the true story, the current financial downturn is having more of a negative impact on women than on men. According to a poll conducted by the American Psychological Association, women are not only reporting more stress than men over finances and the economy, they're also experiencing more stress-related symptoms, such as headaches, fatigue, irritability, and depression. In fact, in all categories polled—money, the economy, job stability, housing costs, and health problems affecting their families—women reported feeling more stress than did men.[21]

In addition, a study conducted by the Center for Work-Life Policy found that although men and women both feel stressed at work, women feel disproportionate stress related to their families' well-being. Why? Because women see a direct link between the time they spend at work and the negative effects on their families (e.g., more junk food, more time in front of a TV, less parental supervision), whereas men tend to blame external factors (e.g., "society," television violence, bad peer groups).[22] And as more women become breadwinners, these stress levels are likely to increase.

What does all this mean for high-achieving women in the world today? It means you're in the race of your life. Being a high-achieving woman puts you squarely in the line of fire for stress and stress-related illnesses. As noted previously, high stress levels are associated with greater risks for depression, anxiety, and other types of emotional problems, as well as serious diseases, including heart disease, high blood pressure, and diabetes. High stress levels also increase the risk for family conflict, domestic violence, child abuse, divorce, and psychological problems for children in the family.

But the good news is that you're not a helpless passenger in a car that's spinning out of control. Although it may not seem like it when you're feeling stressed or burned out, you're in the driver's seat. The course is challenging, yes, but it's manageable. The trick is knowing how to manage it, and that's where our journey begins.

Chapter 2

ROAD CONDITIONS:
Workplace Stressors That
Lead to Burnout

Road Conditions: *information provided to travelers about existing conditions on roadways that can make driving hazardous.*

—from weather.com

When high-achieving women set out on the road to success, they see wide open spaces, opportunities to grow, challenges to be tackled, and chances to make a difference. They're confident. They're energized. They're eager to jump onto the track and race toward the victory flag. They are looking for that moment when all their hard work will finally pay off, the moment they can climb to the top of the podium and look down at the cheering crowd, thinking, "I did it!"

And why would they see it any other way? In the last few decades, women have been told time and time again that they can be anything they want to be. That the days of gender inequality and gender stereotypes are succumbing to a new way of thinking in the workplace, where women are viewed as valuable assets that add to the diversity of the workforce and make it better. That the cracks in the glass ceiling are growing larger each day, allowing more and more women to advance to positions of leadership and increased power. And while none of that is a lie, it's not the whole truth either.

Yes, women are advancing. The examples described in chapter 1 are evidence of that. You're evidence of that. But the journey there and the roads that lie ahead are filled with obstacles, obstacles that many high-achieving women don't expect and frankly aren't prepared for.

The AFL-CIO proudly displays on its Web site the phrase "Working people built America—its buildings, institutions, cultures, and values."[1] The truth, however, is that working *men* built America's institutions. It was their

31

cultures and their values that shaped the structure of our institutions, and for the most part, they still do today. This is certainly part of the problem. As a society, we have not done enough to prepare women for the realities of working in companies whose organizational structure is built around a model that no longer exists, developed at a time in our history when men were the sole breadwinners and women were responsible for homemaking and child rearing. It's a model that is no longer functional for most families today. In fact, families in which the man is the sole provider are now the exception rather than the rule. Yet many businesses are reluctant to give up this outdated model, a decision that often creates enormous stress not only for high-achieving women but for their families as well.

Another part of the problem is that high-achieving women don't think in terms of obstacles. They're highly competitive, they're highly driven, and they want to succeed. So they work tirelessly to reach the top and achieve their "everything I ever wanted" moment. If there is debris on their road, they'll do whatever is necessary to get past it. Obstacles aren't seen as obstacles; they're seen as challenges that need to be overcome. And that's a good thing—except that few anticipate the magnitude and the resistance of the obstacles they'll encounter on their road to success and how much those obstacles will wear them down.

STRESS IN THE WORKPLACE: PERCEPTIONS

With a focus on the bottom line, many workers perceive their companies and those who run them as cold and indifferent. Infamous scandals and blatant fraud committed by wealthy businessmen such as Kenneth Lay and Bernie Madoff have created a pervasive sense of mistrust in the work community at large. This mistrust is further fueled by the huge bonuses paid to a select few top-level executives in banking and other industries, industries that are viewed as at least partially responsible for the recent recession, while the majority of employees struggle to make ends meet.

Job security also looms large in the minds of many of today's workers, especially during today's troubled economic times, when it is clear that no one is immune to layoffs. Even those at the top, with healthy salaries and benefits packages, often worry about job security, fearing that they may be too much of a financial burden for their company to bear. Making matters worse, technology increases the demands placed on workers, who feel constant pressure to respond quickly to e-mail, cell phone, and text messages. This feeling of always being "on call" can lead to frustration, dissatisfaction, and a sense of helplessness—all of which are precursors to burnout.

STRESS IN THE WORKPLACE: REALITIES

Inadequate or Reduced Resources

Budget cuts, as we've recently seen in almost all areas of the workforce, reduce the resources workers need to perform their jobs to the best of their abilities. Teachers, healthcare providers, law enforcement officers, emergency service workers, attorneys—just about everyone across the board seems to be affected, and few professions today feel they have sufficient resources to provide the services expected of them.

Margo, a first-grade public school teacher, describes it this way: "Most of my students come from underprivileged homes. They can't even bring in paper and pencils, so the school has to provide their supplies, which takes away money from other basic things that are supposed to be in first-grade classrooms, like construction paper and art supplies. I feel like it's something my students should have, so I go out and buy extra supplies, but on my salary, it puts more financial stress on me and my family, and that's hard."

Fears

Even those who have sufficient resources often experience stress just trying to hold on to what they have. In a distressed economy, as many have seen firsthand, nothing is certain. Not only are workers worried about layoffs, they're worried about pay cuts and loss of benefits. For many, it's as if the Sword of Damocles is hanging over their heads. And high earners, those making six figures and above, are not immune. In fact, in many cases, they have even more to worry about. Usually, the higher up the ladder employees go, the more hours they are expected to work. For some, the workday never seems to end. In addition, these individuals, their families, and their lifestyles are often dependent on their salaries and benefits. Without them, they would have to make huge lifestyle changes—and they know it. This can affect their mood, state of mind, and, in some cases, their ability to enjoy what they have.

Increasingly Demanding Workloads

Workloads are getting out of control these days. Unfortunately, the reasons behind this surge are not likely to change anytime soon. One reason behind increased workloads is that many companies are hiring fewer employees, either because they simply don't have enough money in their budgets or because they're trying to cut costs, or both. This can not only cause stress levels to soar but also have a significant impact on the services that employees are able to provide to their clients and customers.

There is no better example of this increase in workload than in public defenders' and prosecutors' offices across the country. Due to severe cuts in the government's budget, many of these publicly funded offices have been under hiring freezes for years, resulting in fewer attorneys to handle increasingly high caseloads. It has gotten so bad in some areas that public defenders have actually petitioned the court to withdraw from cases on ethical grounds, arguing that their excessive caseloads prevent them from competently representing their clients. In fact, lawsuits have been filed in several states over this issue.

When attorneys can't keep up with their overwhelming caseloads, their stress levels increase. And because they have to ask for more continuances, court dockets can become backlogged, which can lead to increased stress for judges and other court employees. The stress trickles down and, in the end, everyone suffers.

Another reason for increased workloads is that companies are no longer hiring as many support workers. In many ways, technological advances have made this possible. For instance, some companies feel that professional workers, through the use of today's advanced technology, should be able to handle what traditionally has been considered support work, such as letter writing, data entry, and phone calls. As a result, high-level employees may feel "maxed out" because they don't have sufficient support staff to help them with what seems to be a never-ending list of duties and responsibilities. In fact, in a survey of "extreme" job holders (workers who work long hours in highly demanding jobs), 66 percent of respondents reported that they do not have adequate staffing to manage their workload, and 71 percent said that they do not have a dedicated assistant.[2]

Making the situation worse, many employees feel they have to work faster in order to keep from being buried by the incessant incoming amount of work. Naturally, the faster they work, the more pressure and stress they're likely to feel. Because speed can reduce quality, many high-achieving workers who pride themselves on high-quality work end up feeling dissatisfied with their own output. And contrary to what many people believe, technology doesn't necessarily improve the situation. In fact, although commonly viewed as a faster and more efficient way to increase productivity, technology can actually decrease productivity in many instances, leaving workers feeling frustrated and overwhelmed by more work than most can manage in any given day.

Work Hours

For many workers, nine-to-five workdays are a relic of the past. More employees than ever before are working nights and weekends just to keep up with their job demands. Studies have consistently found that upper-level employees rarely work forty-hour weeks. In fact, in a recent survey conducted by NFI Research, 90 percent of senior executives and managers reported that they work forty-one hours or more in a typical week. Forty percent said that ten hour days are typical.[3] Similar results were obtained by researchers at the Center for Work-Life Policy. Their survey found that 62 percent of extreme job holders work more than fifty hours a week; 35 percent work more than sixty hours a week; and 10 percent work more than eighty hours a week. For many, these hours have increased substantially over the last five years; close to half of all respondents reported that they're working close to seventeen hours more per week than they were five years ago.[4]

More Supervision

Another factor that adds to job stress is that, generally speaking, the higher the position, the more staff that has to be supervised. More people equates to more personalities and more communication styles, all of which need to be effectively understood and managed in order to maintain the respect and the control of the staff. Communication is the hallmark of human interaction. When it breaks down, it can seem like you're alone in a foreign country, unable to speak the language. This often leads to frustration and increased stress for both the employee and the supervisor, as well as unresolved conflicts among coworkers—which in turn increases stress not only because conflict is stressful but also because tension among coworkers removes a buffer that has consistently been found to be an important source of relief from job stress: collegial support.

Policy Constraints

Constraints placed on employees by policies and procedures that affect their work are commonly cited as one of the primary causes of stress and burnout in the workplace. Therapists who work with managed-care companies provide a good example of how these constraints often play out. Although it's the therapist who is actually treating the patient—directly witnessing the severity of the symptoms and the unique circumstances affecting the patient's life—it's usually not the therapist who makes the decision about how many therapy sessions the patient should receive. Those decisions are made by employees of managed-care companies, employees who have never even met the patient. For instance, the managed-care company may approve only ten sessions for a patient, even though the therapist believes that twenty (or more) sessions are necessary. In the end, it's the insurance company that usually wins, leaving many therapists feeling frustrated by policy constraints that seem out of their control.

Inequity

Another frequently cited cause for stress in the workplace is unfair treatment. A variety of situations can give rise to feelings of inequity, but the most common include promotions and salaries. And although men can be victims of inequity on the job, this issue is particularly relevant to women. For instance, when women are promoted to leadership positions, they're usually required to take on more job responsibilities, deal with more conflict, and work longer hours, yet their pay tends to be lower than that of their male counterparts. Unequal pay is a common problem for women in the workforce and is often a source of stress because of its inherent unfairness.

In her book *Why Women Should Rule the World*, former White House press secretary Dee Dee Myers tells of her experience with this situation when she worked for former president Bill Clinton. About a year and a half into her job, Myers learned that one of the deputies in another office at the White House was earning more money than she was, despite the fact that she outranked him and had more responsibilities than he did. She went to Leon Panetta, who was White House chief of staff at the time, to rectify the situation, but she didn't get quite the reaction she expected. Myers writes that she told Panetta that the salary inequity wasn't fair, "but there wasn't a smidgeon of give in Panetta's position. 'Look, we have to pay people based on previous experience and salary history. Plus, he's got a family. It's not going to happen.' The meeting was over. I couldn't believe what I'd just heard. And I was livid."[5]

I suspect she was more than just livid. In fact, I suspect it was stress like this, combined with many other examples of inequity she experienced as the first female White House press secretary, that led to her resignation just two years after she accepted the position.

Lack of Reinforcement and Recognition

"It seems like I just give and give and give, and they just take and take and take," says Sharon, a therapist who works with court-referred substance abusers at a residential treatment center. "I feel guilty for saying it, because when I came into this profession five years ago, I really thought I could help people. But these days I feel like they couldn't care less if I'm here or if I die. I've been laughed at, spit on, and cursed out more times than you can imagine. If they don't care, why should I?"

Sharon's sentiments are common to those who work in helping professions, but these feelings may also arise in other professions when bosses don't acknowledge good work or when pay raises are scarce or nonexistent. However, what can be even worse than a lack of external reinforcement is when stress and frustration build to the point where employees no longer feel intrinsically rewarded by their work. This is the point Sharon was at when I first spoke with her. Within a few months, she decided to leave her job to teach at a university, a decision she later described as the best she'd ever made.

Conflicting Values

Another stressful experience many workers run into on the job is when their value system clashes with what their job requires or expects. Jobs that mislead people, jobs where workers are asked to lie, and jobs where workers are expected to cover up mistakes or violations of policy or law (such as sexual harassment or the falsification of records) are examples of situations that can lead to value conflicts. Although quitting may seem like the only solution in these circumstances, it often isn't that simple, especially when jobs are hard to come by or if the employee can't find another job that would match her current salary. As a result, workers sometimes stay in jobs that they feel compromise their integrity because they feel that they have no other options.

Harassment and Abuse

Harrassment and abuse are often the most harmful stressors employees can suffer in the workplace. These types of pressures can take three forms: psychological, physical, and sexual.

1. **Psychological Abuse:** Psychological abuse in the workplace can be extremely stressful and can have devastating consequences on an employee's self-esteem and self-confidence. Psychological abuse usually takes the form of repetitive berating and degradation by a supervisor or someone who has power over the worker. The worker, for financial or other reasons, often feels powerless to put an end to the abuse by making a complaint or by quitting.
2. **Physical Abuse:** Although physical abuse is not widely reported in employee/employer situations, many workers are exposed to physical abuse through the people they come in contact with on the job (e.g., law enforcement officers), clients they represent (e.g., lawyers), or clients they care for or treat (e.g., mental health and medical providers, social service workers, emergency medical service personnel). Such experiences take away the basic sense of safety that is present in the workplaces of most people and can significantly add to the daily stress these workers experience. They must contend with not knowing if or when, on any given day, they might be attacked, seriously injured, or, in some instances, even killed.

3. **Sexual Abuse or Sexual Harassment:** Of the three forms of abuse, sexual abuse and sexual harassment are probably the most devastating and stressful experiences workers can face on the job. Although sexual harassment can take many forms, the most commonly cited examples are unwanted sexual attention, sexual advances, sexual coercion, and/or the use of sexually crude words, actions, or gestures that create a hostile or offensive work environment. Although there are laws to protect workers from sexual abuse and sexual harassment, many employees are reluctant to report these experiences, which can go on for years, often at the expense of the victim's sense of safety in and out of the work environment, her physical health, her psychological well-being, and her sense of self-worth.

In addition to the often devastating psychological consequences of these abuses, which may include the development of Posttraumatic Stress Disorder, victims may also experience reduced productivity, poorer performance, increased absenteeism, and a stressful or tense work environment.

EXTREME JOBS

The stressors just described are certainly enough to lead to burnout, but if you want to get on the fast track to burnout, try an "extreme job." Extreme jobs are so labor intensive and demanding that they push the limits of even the highest of the high achievers. In fact, economist and consultant Sylvia Ann Hewlett calls these jobs "the American dream on steroids."[6]

Playing off the concept of extreme sports (a media term used to describe highly physical or inherently dangerous activities, such as kickboxing and ice climbing), extreme jobs are those in which employees earn high salaries, work at least sixty hours a week, and work in positions characterized by at least five of the following:

- Physical presence at work at least ten hours a day
- Heavy traveling
- Fast-paced work under tight deadlines
- Unpredictable work flow
- Inordinate scope of responsibility that amounts to more than one job

- Work-related events beyond regular work hours
- Availability to clients 24/7
- Responsibility for profit and loss
- Responsibility for mentoring and recruiting
- Large number of direct reports[7]

Although those who pursue these types of jobs may do so for their own psychological reasons (a reflection of their character, commitment, or stamina; proof of their self-worth, etc.), Hewlett and her colleagues note that organizational changes, communication technology, globalization, and a society that embraces extremes have propelled extreme jobs from a rarity to something fairly common. In fact, in the United States, 21 percent of high-earning workers meet the definition for an extreme job holder. In global companies, the figure climbs to a whopping 45 percent.[8]

Even more surprising is the fact that these jobs are not held primarily by the young and the restless. Hewlett's data indicate that, both globally and in the United States, over half of extreme jobs are held by people between the ages of forty-five and sixty—an age at which many people count on slowing down to enjoy the fruits of their hard labor.[9] This obviously is not the case for extreme job holders, whose average workweek is 72.1 hours.[10]

Although Hewlett's study found that few women hold extreme jobs, those who do may feel an added burden. Because these women are the exception in a group of exceptions, they sometimes feel extra pressure to take on all the challenges their extreme jobs offer and to not complain about the fast pace, long hours, and performance pressures. As Alex, a high-powered corporate attorney, describes it: "When you're running with the big dogs, you can't whine like a Chihuahua when one of them reaches over and bites you." And high-achieving women certainly didn't get where they are by whining. They asked for it, they got it, they love it (to a point), and they want to keep it. So they take the good with the bad and they don't complain, which only adds to their stress levels.

And, as is usually the case for high-achieving women, all is not fair between genders either, even in cases of extreme jobs. Making the burden even more difficult is the fact that, unlike men who hold extreme jobs, women are much less likely to have the support of an at-home spouse. According to Hewlett's survey, the number of men with an at-home spouse is more than double that of women who have this luxury.[11]

GENDER AND STRESS

At this point, you might be thinking that successful men face a lot of these same stressors in the workplace. Does this mean that women don't handle stress as well as men? The answer is *no*.

Groundbreaking research out of UCLA revealed that although women tend to respond to stress differently than men do, our reactions to normal stressful situations are actually much healthier than those of men. This landmark study found that while men generally react to stress with the classic "fight or flight" response, women's reactions typically follow a "tend and befriend" pattern. Specifically, the study found that women tend to respond to stress with behaviors that involve taking care of our children, affiliating with friends, and building and nurturing networks with other women.[12]

Along with other similar findings, this suggests that while men fight back, bottle it up, or isolate themselves during times of stress, women tend to reach out to others, come together, and talk about it—all behaviors that are considered much healthier ways to cope with stress. However, even though we may be biologically programmed to have healthier responses to stress, this advantage is often attenuated by the depth and breadth of the stressors we are exposed to in the workplace and beyond.

GENDER-BASED STRESSORS

The multitude of stressors in the workplace may, in part, explain why only 45 percent of American workers are satisfied with their jobs, a significant drop from the 61 percent of workers who said they were satisfied in 1987.[13] However, the stressors described above account for only part of the stress high-achieving women experience in the workplace. In fact, gender-based workplace stress is often the most difficult to cope with, particularly because it's usually invisible.

Double Binds

A double bind is a dilemma in which a person is presented with two contradictory messages or choices, making the dilemma impossible to resolve. The term *double bind* was coined by anthropologist and social scientist Gregory Bateson and his colleagues. According to their theory, several critical components must be present for a double bind to be effective.[14] One component is that the "bind" must involve two or more people: one (or more) who sends the message and one who is the "victim." Another component is that the direct message presented to the victim must be a contradiction of some sort. For example, the "sender" may say, "Don't let me have another drink before our meeting. If you do, I'm going to be angry with you." That message is then followed by a secondary, contradictory message, often conveyed by a tone or posture. This secondary message typically implies that if the sender of the message was important to the victim (e.g., the victim loved, cared about, wanted to please the sender), the victim would let the sender have another drink. Often, this bind makes the victim feel as if she can't comment on or acknowledge the contradiction. The final two components of a double bind are that it repeats itself over time, and the victim isn't able to "escape" the situation, usually because some relationship binds the victim to the sender.[15]

Due to the nature and structure of most workplaces, women are more likely than men to experience double binds on the job. Using the example above, if the employee allows her boss to have a drink before the meeting, he'll be angry. But if she doesn't allow him to have a drink, he'll still be angry. It's a classic no-win situation.

A common double bind experienced by women in the workplace is related to how leadership is judged. "Good" leaders are expected to be strong, confident, and assertive. However, when women act in strong, confident, and assertive ways, they tend to be perceived as uncaring, self-promoting, and aggressive—all of which are negative descriptors. But when they act in more collaborative ways, they're viewed as not having "good" leadership skills.

According to Catalyst, a leading research and advisory organization that works with businesses to expand opportunities for working women, "[t]hese polarized perceptions [about leadership] represent a type of 'all-or-none' thinking that does not apply to men in leadership roles."[16] And the consequences are steep. Not only do these perceptions negatively affect women's advancement, they impact salaries, perceived status among coworkers, and a woman's overall sense of security and safety in a company.

Gender Stereotypes

Gender stereotypes are false representations or misrepresentations of reality based on gender that unconsciously govern our thoughts and actions, even though we typically do not acknowledge them. Catalyst describes the underlying process of stereotyping as follows: "Because most people are not aware of how their thinking and behavior are automatically influenced by stereotypes, they conclude their perceptions come from objective observations. This is why stereotyping is so difficult to address—we all do it, but we often don't realize or believe that we do."[17] As a result, gender stereotypes have the potential to become "a powerful yet invisible threat to women leaders and the organizations in which they work and lead," which can cause their impact to be underestimated.[18] In fact, one of the most challenging problems with gender stereotypes is that they're hard to detect and even harder to control. Rarely are these inaccurate "judgments" openly discussed by others, which can create "invisible barriers" that impede women's advancement.[19]

Impact of Stereotypes and Double Binds on Women in the Workplace

Gender stereotypes can have a significant impact on the way working women are viewed by their colleagues, as well as their chances for advancement. For example, women are generally viewed as being better at "taking care" skills—supporting and encouraging others—while men are generally seen as having better "take charge" skills, such as solving problems, displaying assertiveness, and influencing supervisors.[20] Although these views are often inaccurate, the fact that they exist color the way both males and females are judged in the workplace.

Furthermore, while both of these qualities—taking care and taking charge—may in fact make a good leader, the reality is that the stereotypical masculine traits tend to be considered important, often essential components of effective leadership (note that I'm referring here to leadership as defined historically by men). That is, assertiveness and problem-solving skills are viewed as being more consistent with leadership, whereas being supportive and encouraging is viewed as more consistent with being a follower. As a result, women seeking leadership positions usually have to work much harder than male candidates to "prove" they possess the stereotypical masculine leadership skills. In addition, women often have to overcome the inaccurate perception that because they may excel at supporting and encouraging others, they can't excel at other things, such as leading, problem solving, and being competitive.[21] And again, these perceptions themselves—that women are more supportive and men are more influential and assertive—are often inaccurate anyway.

Gender stereotypes and double binds often work hand in hand. For example, when a woman's job performance is measured in stereotypical ways, it often places her in a double bind. Studies have shown that when women act in ways that are consistent with gender stereotypes (e.g., supportive, encouraging), they tend to be judged as more personable and therefore are better liked, yet they are seen as less competent. When they act in ways that are inconsistent with gender stereotypes (e.g., assertive, strong, problem solvers), they tend to be judged as competent but overly aggressive and not likable.[22]

Another common double bind faced by high-achieving working mothers is described by Pamela Stone in her book *Opting Out*. Stone writes, "In operating as a barrier to women's continued employment once they become mothers, workplace inflexibility in high-status professional jobs is the 'hard place' of the double bind. Double binds present contradictions and inconsistencies. How do women reconcile their aspirations with their experiences? How do they make sense of professions that, on the one hand, appear to welcome them, confer considerable status upon them, and are an important part of their identity and, on the other hand, seem to pull back the welcome mat, marginalize them, and force them to compromise their other important identity as mothers?"[23]

Naturally, such binds can lead to feelings of frustration and anger. But when women express feelings of anger and frustration on the job, they're often labeled as overly emotional or seen as unable to handle the stress of the more demanding position. Because these judgments are typically internalized and not directly expressed, they're difficult to detect and difficult to combat. And more often than not, it's this inability to control what is happening that little by little wears down high-achieving women and ultimately makes them prime targets for burnout.

However, it's important to recognize that stereotypes and double binds aren't always externally generated. High-achieving women often buy into the same expectations and stereotypes as men do. In fact, research tells us that gender-based views about stereotypical feminine traits and stereotypical masculine traits are prevalent among *both* genders.[24] This means that women are equally as likely as men to judge women who are assertive as "bossy" or "bitchy" and men who are assertive as "strong, competent leaders."

In addition, women sometimes create double binds for themselves—in fact, it's actually quite common among high-achieving women. Here's an example: "I should take that extra assignment because if I do, my boss will give me more responsibilities" (or a promotion, praise, a raise, etc.) or "If I don't take that extra assignment, John will take it and my boss will see him as more capable" (or dedicated or competent, etc.). But then comes the bind: "If I take that extra assignment, I won't be able to get my other assignments turned in as quickly, which is going to make my boss see me as incompetent" (or lazy or not dedicated enough or not able to juggle as many balls as John). This type of scenario repeats itself over and over in the lives of competitive, ambitious women and creates, as my daughter describes it, "an internal angst that lashes at the soul." In other words . . . stress.

Communication Styles

In 1995, Deborah Tannen wrote *Talking from 9 to 5: Women and Men at Work*, a book that describes the "typical" styles of female and male communication and how these styles can impact the dynamics of the workplace.[25] Tannen's research, which spans more than three decades, is widely cited in the literature on communication styles and how differences in the way people communicate can lead to misunderstandings and conflict. As such, her work fits in well with discussions related to common sources of stress in the workplace. However, because Tannen's most recent book focuses on *gender* differences, whenever I cite it in discussions related to high-achieving women, the argument inevitably follows that (a) not all women (or men for that matter) fit the "typical" descriptions, and (b) by describing what is "typical," we encourage the same stereotypes that were just described.

First, let me say that (a) is definitely true. And Tannen agrees. As she notes in *Talking from 9 to 5*, "it is critical to bear in mind that the influence of gender is just one of the many influences, and that patterns are just that— patterns to which individuals may adhere more or less or not at all, not templates that can be placed over every individual, as if each of us could be stuffed into a single mold."[26] In fact, the large majority of the high-achieving women with whom I've worked over the years think and communicate in ways that Tannen and others would describe as "more typical" of men. So, again, what may be "typical" for *most* women doesn't necessarily apply to what is "typical" for you or for other high-achieving women.

With respect to (b), while it is true that some people misuse typical patterns of thinking or behavior by rigidly applying them to all members of a particular group (women do this, rich people do that, etc.), it doesn't mean that we should completely ignore patterns. The fact is that there often *are* real differences in the way women and men communicate. With that said, though, it's also the case that there often are differences in the way women communicate with other women, and men communicate with other men, and parents communicate with children, and Europeans communicate with Americans, and New Yorkers communicate with Californians, and the wealthy communicate with the poor—I could go on and on. Tannen agrees with this as well. "Although I may talk about 'women' and 'men,'" she writes in *Talking from 9 to 5*, "I am always aware, and remind readers to be aware that . . . gender [again] is only one of the many influences on conversational style. Each individual has a unique style, influenced by a personal history of many influences such as geographic region, ethnicity, class, sexual orientation, occupation, religion, and age—as well as a unique personality and spirit."[27]

Clearly it's not as simple as women's communication styles being different from men's. If that were the case, women would never have problems communicating with other women, and men would never have problems communicating with other men. Each gender would always be on the same sheet of music, so to speak, while mixed-gender conversations would never be harmonious. But we know that's not the case.

So although there is a large amount of literature that discusses gender differences in communication, I generally don't find it useful—especially with respect to high-achieving women—to break the styles down into what women *tend* to do and what men *tend* to do. My advice to you is to try to figure out what *you* tend to do, and use that information to understand how your communication style may be affecting your relationships and your stress level at work (or anywhere else, for that matter). To facilitate this, I've chosen to describe communication styles, as much as possible, in gender-neutral terms. But before we get into specific styles, there are a few other important caveats to keep in mind.

First, remember that *communication style* refers only to how certain people are *likely* to think, communicate, and behave, not to how they *always* will think, communicate, and behave. For example, when I'm snacking, I tend to gravitate more toward candy than chips. Does that mean I always eat candy and never eat chips? Does that mean I love sugar and hate salt? No, it's just a tendency, meaning I'm more likely to do it. The same applies to styles of communication.

Second, it's important to recognize that communication styles exist along a continuum. Consider the style of directness as an example. Some people are so direct in their communication that they're viewed as uncaring and insensitive. Others are so indirect that it's impossible to figure out what they're trying to say. And then there are those at all points in between. Few people will be at the extreme ends of any of the continuums, although for illustrative purposes, it may sometimes appear that way.

Finally, the way we "typically" think, communicate, and act is often affected by what is going on around us. In other words, how we communicate is not set in stone. Someone may be soft-spoken, unassertive, and not easily angered most of the time. However, if you put her in a situation where her child is being threatened, you're likely to see a very different reaction. There are less extreme examples as well, such as people who are very talkative in small groups but practically mute in large groups. The point is, typical communication styles sometimes change depending on the circumstances.

With these points in mind, let's turn to communication styles, which, for illustrative purposes, I've broken down into a few broad, polarized categories.[28] As you'll come to see, the greatest risk for misunderstanding and conflict occurs when coworkers or colleagues are at divergent ends of these continuums.[29]

Competitive vs. Affiliative: Some individuals are highly invested in the position they hold both in their peer groups and in the power structure of the organizations for which they work. As such, they do their best to avoid situations in which their "status" in the power hierarchy might be compromised. In other words, they try to avoid being in a position of weakness or in situations in which they feel inferior to another person, commonly referred to as a "one-down" position.

These individuals tend to be oriented toward competitiveness, power, and dominance, and their communication style tends to be directed toward accomplishing these goals. These are people who like to make the decisions, and they make them with confidence. Their communication style tends to be more direct, assertive, and challenging. They often use direct challenges to flush out weaknesses in plans or ideas. If those who are being challenged can support their ideas, plans, or arguments—or better yet, if they can come up with superior ones—that's fine. But if they can't, these competitive communicators will call them on it, often taking pride in the fact that they discovered the flaws before the plan or idea took root.[30] Because these types of behaviors are commonly associated with competence, strength, and confidence, individuals with a more competitive style are often at an advantage when it comes to being recognized and promoted at work.[31]

On the other hand, there are individuals who aren't particularly interested in competition, power, or dominance. They have more of a supportive and collaborative style of communicating and tend to see direct challenges and open disagreements as aggressive, hostile, and often personal.[32] They are more comfortable bringing people together, sharing power, viewing everyone as having something worthwhile to share, and working out the "rules" together.[33] In fact, they don't like to see anyone in a one-down position and will often try to bring up those who are down, or they themselves will come down to the other person's level.

While there is nothing wrong with either style—in fact, both are likely to be advantageous at different times in different situations—workers with more affiliative styles tend to be at a disadvantage in work environments where leadership is traditionally defined (i.e., strong, powerful, assertive) and where the power structure is hierarchical (where there is a clear chain of command) as opposed to horizontal (where the power is more evenly distributed and shared).[34] They are less likely to get recognized for their contributions and may have more difficulty getting promoted.[35]

In addition, it's important to remember that women, regardless of the style they gravitate toward, are often not judged the same as men who have the same style. As Tannen explains, "Women are expected to hedge their beliefs as opinions, to seek opinions and advice from others, to be 'polite' in their requests. If a woman talks this way, she is seen as lacking in authority. But if she talks with certainty, makes bold statements of fact rather than hedged statements of opinion, interrupts others, goes on at length, and speaks in a declamatory and aggressive manner, she will be disliked."[36]

Decisive vs. Inquisitive: For reasons similar to the ones noted above, some people are not comfortable asking questions or they see no need to do so, particularly in situations where asking may suggest a lack of knowledge or be viewed as a sign of weakness. These individuals tend to simply listen to whatever information is presented to them and make their decisions then and there, even if the information they have is minimal or incomplete. They then give out orders or directions and expect them to be followed with little or no discussion or debate. If they have questions, they either find out the answers on their own or make mistakes and hopefully learn from them.[37]

Conversely, there are some individuals who prefer to have as much information and input from others as possible before they make their decisions. They have no qualms about asking questions and they like to know what other people think before they decide on a course of action. Involving others in the process is done not only to get more information but also to facilitate feelings of collegiality. As a result, their styles of communicating are generally viewed as more inquisitive and inclusive.

In the workplace, individuals with more inclusive styles are generally thought of as caring and friendly. Yet they also tend to be viewed as indecisive and unsure of themselves. While this is not accurate in many cases, the perception puts these workers at a disadvantage in workplaces that place a higher value on decisiveness, even if the decisions are ill informed and unsound due to lack of information.[38]

Accomplishments vs. Connections: Some individuals are very comfortable taking credit for their work and accepting praise and rewards when they're offered. They are not the least bit shy about letting others know about their accomplishments.[39] When they're making a presentation about something they've done, they're more likely to use "I" than "we" and are more likely to take full credit for their work.[40] Although some of these individuals are braggarts, many of them are simply people who take pride in their accomplishments and enjoy when their hard work is recognized.

In contrast, some people feel very uncomfortable stepping up and taking credit for what they've done. They're more invested in maintaining connections with others and are therefore more likely to use "we" when presenting their work and are more likely to give at least partial credit to other people, even when the work is all their own.[41]

There are benefits to both styles; however, in the majority of workplaces, those who make their accomplishments known and take full credit for their work are likely to be at a distinct advantage when it comes to awards, bonuses, recognition, and promotions.

Direct vs. Indirect: If you need something done, there are two basic ways you can communicate that need: directly or indirectly. Direct communicators simply state what they need. Polite direct communicators may convey their message with an added "please" and "thank you," but there isn't much room for confusion when your boss says, "Get me a blue pen."

On the other hand, indirect communication is ripe for confusion, misunderstanding, and frustration on both sides.[42] An indirect communication may be as vague as "They like for me to sign the requisition in blue ink," or it may be a little less indirect, such as "It would help if I had a blue pen." The first example is simply a statement, making it hard for the receiver of the message to know if there is a need behind the statement. The latter suggests that there might be a need for a blue pen. However, it's certainly not a direct request.

Few people go around barking direct orders whenever they need something. Almost everyone uses both direct and indirect forms of communication throughout the day. However, most people lean toward one end of the continuum or the other.

Within reason, both forms of communication have their place in the workplace. However, when the two styles collide, there is often a great deal of tension for all involved. Those who use more direct means of communicating are more likely to offend those who are less direct, while those who favor indirect speech are likely to be an ongoing source of frustration for those who prefer directness. In fact, when the different styles aren't understood, it opens the door for frustration and, in some cases, hostility on both sides of the equation. For example, from more indirect communicators, I've heard the "other side" described as loud, obnoxious, Hitler-like assholes (and a few other choice words I won't put in print). From direct communicators, I've heard equally negative descriptors, such as scaredy-cats, spineless, annoying, insecure, wimpy, manipulative, and "makes me want to pull my hair out!"

But probably the biggest risk of indirect communication in the workplace is that things don't get done how or when they should. This can go one of two ways. First, when a message is indirect, the receiver may not recognize that anything needs to be handled, so nothing gets done. Second, when a request is unclear, it's much easier to purposely ignore it. In either case, if you are in an occupation where your safety or the safety of others is an issue, such as doctor, nurse, law enforcement officer, air traffic controller, pilot, or firefighter, indirect communication can be dangerous.[43]

The Journey vs. the Final Destination: Some people are more interested in the process—how they or others get to a result. Others are interested only in the final product. For them, how and why the result came to be is irrelevant.

Similarly, there are those who are solution oriented. When a problem is presented, they immediately jump in and try to "fix it." Their focus is on finding a solution. However, some people don't really want a solution when they tell someone about a problem. They simply want to talk about it rather than rush to solve it.[44]

Although neither of these styles is necessarily a major advantage in the workplace, problems can develop if the different styles aren't understood and recognized as equally valid. When people with compatible styles communicate with each other, there usually isn't a problem. But when a "journey" person gets together with a "final destination" person, there is much more room for misunderstandings, conflicts, and frustration.

Joann's story exemplifies this conflict. "When I run into a problem, sometimes I just want to process my thoughts out loud," she says, describing one of her biggest frustrations with her business partner, Mitch. "I don't want him to fix it. I just want him to listen, but without fail, he jumps right in there and solves the problem. It drives me crazy." In these kinds of situations, although the surface problem may get solved, the communication problems linger, adding stress to both sides of the relationship.

Boy Humor vs. Girl Humor: I'm going to go out on a limb on this one and bring gender into the picture because with rare exception have I ever seen or read or heard of differences in styles of humor that cross over gender lines. In fact, because males historically have defined what is funny, it's common to hear men say: "Women don't have a sense of humor."

The reality is that women do have a sense of humor—it just tends to be different from men's.[45] Jokes told by men tend to be shorter with quick punch lines, typically revolving around themes of verbal or physical aggressiveness, insults, and sex—in some cases at the expense of women. Women's jokes tend to be longer, more similar to storytelling than quips or the one-two punch-line jokes. Female humor also tends to be more self-deprecatory and anecdotal, and is often based on personal experiences.[46]

The funny thing is that both genders think what they're saying is funny, but the opposite sex often doesn't get the joke. In fact, women tend to see male humor as mean-spirited, hostile, and personal, while men don't see much humor in self-deprecation.[47] So why is there this disconnect?

Some research suggests that it has to do with the way male and female brains process humor.[48] Other experts say that the differences have a social and psychological basis. English professor Linda Naranjo-Huebl offers several of these theories in her article on women and humor, one of which is that "women, even empowered women who feel relatively free to share their humor, generally do not use male forms of humor . . . because they simply are not the best tool to facilitate their communication goals."[49] She says that because women tend to be more invested in maintaining interpersonal connections than men are, they don't see any benefit in putting other people down. Another theory, supported by Dr. Paul McGhee, a pioneer in humor research, suggests that those in power tend to prefer humor that disparages those who are not in power, whereas those who aren't in power tend to find self-deprecation more humorous. Interestingly, McGhee found one exception: women who do not hold traditional views of gender roles are usually not amused by self-deprecatory humor.[50]

FORGING NEW PATHS

Even when gender is not an issue, stress is very much alive and well in the workplace. Then when we throw in all the gender-specific stressors—stereotypical performance measures, double binds, gender-biased judgments of competence, inability to vent for fear of appearing weak or incapable, longer work hours coupled with domestic responsibilities, and little or no control over these stressors—it's easy to see how we have a perfect setup for a huge, fiery crash. And the worst part is, most high-achieving women never see the embankment coming.

Hopefully, with the help of this book, you will see it coming and will use this knowledge to make changes that will reduce your stress levels and give you the power you need to fight back against workplace stress. Of course, the best way to reduce stress in the workplace is for women and their employers, human resource departments, and coworkers to join together and make changes. Unfortunately, however, organizational changes have been slow in coming, and waiting for change is likely to make your stress worse. This leaves the challenge up to you—to forge new paths, to find solutions that make it easier for you to navigate the bumpy roads. Here are a few ideas that might help.

Knowledge

Although you may not realize it, you've actually taken a huge step toward a solution. To make my point, let's consider the medical field. Doctors and nurses constantly come in contact with sick and infected people, but they themselves are rarely sick. Why?

For one thing, they have a good understanding of how illnesses are transferred and they take preventive measures, such as using gloves, wearing masks, and frequently washing their hands. In addition, they know what symptoms look like, so when they begin to experience certain symptoms, they can quickly begin to treat them. As a result, they are likely to have a speedier recovery. In short, they use the knowledge they have to make changes in their work environments to lessen their chances of getting sick, and when they do start to feel sick, they know what to do to feel better.

You can do the same. In many ways, the workplace is a psychologically sick environment that is constantly trying to pull you in and make you sick, too. By taking positive steps to change your work environment, you can prevent stress from getting to the point where it wears you out and takes you down.

Advocating for Workplace Education and Training

The more aware each worker is of differences in communication styles and why they exist, the more understanding and acceptance there is likely to be of these differences. But one person is rarely in a position to do this alone. If you feel that much of the tension in your workplace is due to communication disconnects, then ask management to bring in speakers to conduct communication training and awareness workshops to help everyone understand, appreciate, and accept differences in communication styles. The best way to improve communication is to understand it and to become more flexible in how you communicate, as well as how you interpret what others say.[51]

Using Communication Styles to Your Advantage

Now that you're aware of the types of communication styles and how they relate to one another, you can experiment with different styles to try to find the right one for your specific circumstances. Easier said than done? Not really. You use different communication styles all the time, often without realizing it.

A good example is how we communicate with children. Most adults know that the likelihood of getting a child to do something depends on how they approach the situation. "Please take the garbage out before you open that bag of chips" (a direct order) is more likely to produce the desired response, as opposed to "Do you mind taking the garbage out?" (a polite question that implies a choice). However, if you are talking to your partner or roommate, the reverse is likely to apply. Adults of equal status in a relationship typically don't respond well to direct orders. This is just one example of how we use different communication styles in different situations to produce a desired behavior. The truth is, we change our communication styles to fit our situations all the time. So why not try it at work?

One way to do this is to think of communication as a dance. If you're both in sync, doing the same dance and hearing the same music, things should go smoothly. But if you're off on even one of those things, you're probably going to get tripped up and stumble over each other. So, let's say your boss has a different communication style than you, and you find that you're bumping into each other a lot. Try switching up your steps a little. If you use more of a "competitive" style when telling your staff what to do and how to do it, and you've been getting resistance, try a different rhythm.

The first step in this process starts with you. You have to figure out what your style is and what styles your coworkers and bosses are using. If you come away from this chapter realizing that part of your frustration is that you feel as if your voice is never heard or that someone else is always taking credit for your ideas, take a look at what your role might be in that dance. Do you freely give or share credit with others when you've done the work your-self? Do you speak in ways that make it seem like you're unsure of yourself? Are you soft-spoken? Are you unnecessarily apologetic? Do you begin sentences with "I'm not sure if this is something you're interested in hearing, but . . ." or "You probably already know this, but . . ." Although there is nothing wrong with these styles per se, in a workplace where the unwritten rules favor those who are assertive, are confident, and like to give orders, you're going to be at a distinct disadvantage.

Once you've analyzed your style, the next step is to figure out where you'd like to be and how you might be able to adjust your communication style to get there. Using the example above, consider moving up a few notches on the assertiveness continuum. This doesn't necessarily mean that you have to overpower the room or blast everyone out. Instead of starting off with "I'm not sure if . . . ," start off more confidently: "I think that the best way to . . ." or "I strongly believe that . . ."

Start off slow. Remember that in any experiment, if you increase the independent variable (the variable that changes) by too much, you may not get a good read on the dependent variable (the impact of the change). In other words, if you change your style too dramatically and you receive a negative reaction, you won't know if a smaller degree of change might have met with better results. So move up or down a particular continuum only a notch or two at a time, and then assess the impact of the change. If it's positive, but not enough for your liking, turn it up a notch. If it's too uncomfortable for you, or you find that the consequences are not worth the benefits, move it down a bit.

But changing yourself is not necessarily the only way this dance can work. For example, when it comes to direct versus indirect styles of communicating, my notch on the "directness" continuum is closer to the "direct" end. Because of this, whenever I hire new staff I tell them right up front that I prefer direct communication—if you have a new idea, tell me what it is; if a mistake was made, tell me right away so it can be handled; if something is bothering you, speak up and let me know; if I see that you're doing something wrong, I'm going to address it with you directly and I'd like you to do the same. In fact, I tell staff this even before I hire them to better ensure that they'll be a good fit with my style and with that of the rest of the staff. Inevitably, though, I will hire someone who says she is perfectly fine with direct communication, yet she isn't.

Joan, a secretary in my practice, is a good example. A few weeks after she was hired, she came into my office and asked, "I was wondering how much time it should take to get everything done that you give me?" Since I don't stand over my employees with a stopwatch, I knew she was trying to tell me something, but I wasn't sure what it was. Was she trying to gauge how quickly she was working compared to someone else in the practice? Did she finish everything I gave her and now wanted praise? Was she not able to get to all the work I had given her? Did she think her workload was too heavy? Was she asking for help? I had no idea. Her communication style was too indirect.

So I asked Joan why she was asking the question. "Well, the phones were very busy today," she answered. Hmm. An indirect question and an equally indirect answer. Although the answer put me a little closer to what she was trying to tell me, I didn't want to assume anything, nor did I want to reinforce that type of indirect communication with a new employee. So I reminded Joan that I work best with direct communication and explained that if she needed help with something, she needed to be more direct in what that was. I also added, much to her relief, that she was new and that I understood it was going to take her a little while to get up to speed.

As it turns out, Joan hadn't been able to get everything done that was assigned to her that day because the volume of phone calls was heavier than usual. Once she realized that her job wasn't in jeopardy, she explained that she wasn't sure if it was her work pace or if it was just the nature of the job, so she approached the subject indirectly. This was understandable, but it was also the case that Joan's overall style was much more indirect than mine. In time, Joan adjusted to my style, with occasional reminders on my part whenever she veered too far in the "indirect" direction.

I use this example to show that there is more than one way things can "move" when you're talking about communication styles. In some cases, especially if you're the boss or the supervisor, it's okay to try to see if your employee/supervisee can learn to move a little closer to your style. Again, the key is being aware of the differences in style so you can first understand what is happening and then try to address it, rather than constantly getting tripped up by a partner who is doing the waltz while you're doing the tango.

This is in no way meant to suggest that you should adopt a communication style that is uncomfortable for you or one that clashes with your values. You shouldn't try to be someone you're not, nor should you join in on something you find offensive, such as crude or sexist humor. If you do, it will likely come across as insincere and superficial anyway. The key is being flexible while at the same time finding something that feels comfortable to you.[52]

At the same time, however, you need to recognize that there may be consequences for becoming more or less assertive, being more or less direct, speaking in a softer or a louder voice, or changing any of the other ways you typically communicate. So if you decide to experiment with some changes, you should think of it as a calculated risk. As Tannen says, "Even Margaret Mead, according to her daughter, Mary Catherine Bateson, judiciously chose the issues on which she would speak up, so as not to come across as dominant. Such a strategy may be a wise one for everyone, women as well as men. On the other hand, it may also be wise to decide that being seen as aggressive is a price worth paying for being listened to."[53]

Handling Double Binds and Gender Stereotypes

Metacommunication: Successfully navigating double binds and stereotypes in the workplace can be challenging, but that doesn't mean they can't be navigated. One of the best ways to do this is to directly comment on the double bind or stereotype rather than allowing it to silently inflict stress. The process of calling attention to a communicated message is called *metacommunication*. It's basically communicating about communication, and it can be a powerful way to reduce the power of a double bind or stereotype.

Metacommunication is done by giving people feedback about the binds they put you in. For example, you might say something like, "I wonder if you realize the situation that puts me in. If I let you have a drink, you're going to get angry. But if I don't let you have the drink, I suspect you're going to be angry with me anyway."

In some cases, you might have more success if you do your metacommunicating privately, with only you and the other person involved in the conversation. But sometimes talking about the issue in a group setting can be effective as well. You need to use your best judgment when deciding which approach to take, considering both potential benefits and potential consequences. You also might have more success if you take more of a "Columbo" approach ("I'm a little confused. This happened and then this happened, and I'm wondering if you realize . . .") as opposed to a confrontational or accusatory approach ("I can't believe you just . . ."). But whichever way you choose to handle the bind, by talking about it, you're basically putting the bind back into the hands of the "sender." In other words, you're removing the implicit agreement of silence between you and the sender, which takes away one of the critical components necessary for a double bind to work— the silence that gives it strength.

Of course, it's unrealistic to expect all senders to recognize the error of their ways, fall on their knees, and beg forgiveness with promises to never bind you up again. And I certainly can't guarantee there won't be any backlash. However, calling attention to something is the first step toward changing it.[54] A sender may well think twice before trying it again, knowing that you're no longer going to silently sit by and let it happen.

A similar form of metacommunication can be used with respect to gender stereotypes. For example, rather than sit there and stew with anger (which just raises your stress level), speak up the moment you hear or see something that you feel is unfair or inaccurate. Again, I'm not promising there won't be any backlash, but the alternative is to prolong the life of something that should have died long ago.

As an example, I was having lunch a while back with a group of attorneys. One of them was talking about how she had spent a week trying to convince the prosecutor in one of her cases that her client should get probation. That day, the prosecutor called to tell her that he was going to agree to the terms of probation she was asking for. One of the male lawyers at the table commented, "That guy has no backbone," referring to the prosecutor. "If you'd have gone in there gangbusters, I bet he'd have given your guy even less time." This clearly didn't sit well with her, and she immediately responded. "Or he'd have put my guy in prison. I'm happy and my client's happy. Just because you might have handled it a different way doesn't make the way I handled it wrong. Sometimes a scalpel is more effective than a sledgehammer." Surprisingly, given that this was a group of mostly male lawyers, there was no retort.

Actions Speak Louder Than Words: Some women take a different approach to gender biases and stereotypes. Instead of commenting directly upon them when they happen, they simply show where their strengths lie and act consistently.[55] For example, a judge shared with me that when she first took the bench, many of the lawyers in her courtroom seemed to think that because she was soft-spoken and a female that she would be a pushover. Her response: "I never addressed it openly. I just did my job every day. I ruled consistently. When the situation called for it, I judged harshly, and when there were extenuating circumstances, I was more lenient. I think if you asked them now, they wouldn't judge me one way or the other. I think they'd say I'm fair."

Separate Who You Are from the Underlying Message: In some cases, the reason double binds and stereotypes cause women so much distress is because they go to the essence of their identity and exacerbate any insecurities they have. This is completely understandable. Few people are so self-confident that they're never affected by anything negative that is said about them. In fact, if that were the case, I'd be much more worried about them than those with normal insecurities. With that said, however, there are times when women are better served by separating their identity from the communication. Instead of taking the message personally, you may be better off focusing on what the messenger is trying to communicate.

For instance, if we go back to the "drinking" double bind, the message is more about the sender than it is about the recipient. The double bind may certainly be there, but what is the underlying message? Maybe the boss is using the double bind as a cry for help. He may be saying, "I really want a drink before we go into that meeting and you know if I don't have one I'm going to sound like an anxious, blubbering idiot. If you cared about me, you'd help me get help for my drinking problem." Seeing the double bind from this perspective sometimes reduces its power and, therefore, its impact on you.

Leaving the Race: Another option, albeit a much more dramatic one, is to leave the situation that is causing the stress. Although this can be extremely difficult, particularly in a bad economy, there are some workplaces that are so toxic that the only way to survive is to leave.

Obviously, a decision such as this should never be made lightly, impulsively, or in anger. But if, after careful thought and conversations with people you trust, you decide that the situation is irresolvable, the best choice for your future health, happiness, and overall well-being may be to quit or, if possible, ask for a transfer to another department where you believe there are likely to be fewer issues. It's impossible to find a completely stress-free work environment, but you shouldn't have to remain in one that is psychologically abusive or so stressful that it affects your health.

Finally, in cases of sexual abuse and harassment, there is never really a good enough reason to stay and let the abuse continue. Sexual abuse and harassment represent the ultimate abuse of power and control in a relationship. As a result, the abuse rarely stops on its own (unless the perpetrator moves on to another victim, which is equally as bad). Both behaviors are against the law and should be reported. And while I understand that in some situations it's frightening to report abuse, to not do so leaves you and other potential victims at the mercy of someone who has only his (or her, in some situations) own best interests in mind. No job is worth sacrificing your health, safety, and dignity.

LOOKING AHEAD

As more women gain access to upper-level management and executive positions—despite the odds against them—the gender-biased perceptions, images, and definitions that have been held so long about what makes a good leader and what makes someone competent should begin to slowly disappear, making room for more equitable definitions that aren't as dichotomous. In fact, if what sociology professor Kathleen Gerson describes in her book *The Unfinished Revolution* offers a glimpse into the future, women will not be the only agents of change in the future.[56]

According to Gerson, both the men and the women in what she refers to as the "children of the gender revolution"—the generation now moving into the workforce—have high hopes for a world in which they can have a career and a family that are unrestricted by rigid gender roles, and they want a workplace that can provide that.[57] As we look ahead, it is my hope that the diversity of their experiences will shape the workplace into a place where the needs of families and the unique qualities of women will no longer be punished but will be welcomed and embraced.

Chapter 3

ROAR OF THE CROWD:
Societal Stressors That
Lead to Burnout

Roar of the Crowd: *a loud, confused sound made by a group of people shouting together.*
—from BrainyQuote.com

The roar of the crowd. Everyone loves it. Except, of course, when the crowd is booing. And then there are those fickle crowds, the ones that applaud and boo at different times during the performance. Performers hate them. And for high-achieving women, there has never been a crowd more fickle than society.

Conflicting messages abound for women living in today's world, and this is echoed in what high-achieving women face in the workplace. For women caught in these seemingly impossible conflicts, it can feel like society is suffering from Multiple Personality Disorder. One of the personalities sits in the front row of the stands, watching the race, applauding you, rooting you on to victory. Then, as you make your way to the winner's podium, you inadvertently cross over some socially prescribed line, often invisible until after you cross it, and that's when the other personality appears and boos you off the platform.

Kathleen Hall Jamieson describes this phenomenon in her 1995 book *Beyond the Double Bind*. She opens the book with a reference to the witch trials of the 1600s: "In 1631," she writes, "in *Cautio Criminalis*, Julius Friedrich Spee identified one no win situation in which prosecutors placed women accused of witchcraft. The suspect witch was submerged in a pond. If she drowned, she deserved to; if she didn't, she was a witch. In the first case, god was revealing her nature; in the second, the devil."[1] Jamieson goes on to point out, "Three and a half centuries later, the penalties are disdain and financial loss, not death, and the sanctions social, not theological, but it can still be hazardous for a woman to venture out beyond her 'proper sphere.'"[2] Disappointingly, fifteen years later, little has changed.

61

Despite advances toward gender equality, women are still subjected to impossible double standards and double binds by a society that on the one hand seems to have moved beyond rigid gender roles, yet at the same time still ties women to the chains that once bound them. Why do these binds still exist in a society in which women make up not only half of the population but half of the workforce as well? You don't have to look far to find the answer.

Relatively speaking, America is a young country that flourished first by allowing people to practice religions of their choosing, and later by being open to new ideas of government that gave rights to the people to govern themselves rather than to be subjected to the tyrannical reign of royalty. However, the rights of the people were not truly of the *people*. They were the rights of men—white men. They were the only ones who had rights when this country's Constitution and laws were established, so it should come as no surprise that when "the rules" were being decided, there were no women in the room. And even if there had been, they would not have been permitted to speak.

Perpetually demonized for the sins of Eve and portrayed as intellectually inferior to men, women were considered property. They could not vote. They could not keep any money they earned or received. They could not legally enter into a contract. They had one role and one role only—domestic. They were responsible for taking care of the home, taking care of their husbands, and bearing and taking care of their children. But even this last role was tenuous. Although they were primarily responsible for the upbringing of their children, they had no rights over what happened to them. Fathers made the sole decisions as to where the children would live, what they would do or not do, and if the mother disagreed . . . well, too bad. Property has no voice.

In 1848, the first women's rights convention was held in Seneca Falls, New York, but it wasn't until more than seventy years later that women were given the right to vote. Changes began to take place in the nineteenth century, but the fact still remained, as it does today, that the "system"—the societal and institutional "rules" that define how we live and work—were created by men for men. And in many respects, we are still being held to the restrictive rules and roles of long ago.

Motherhood continues to be regarded by society as the quintessential accomplishment of a woman's life. Although "on paper," women have the right to choose, those who choose not to have children continue to be viewed by a large and vocal section of society as somehow betraying their true destiny—and these voices are not just men's. Many women hold this view as well.

It was only a few decades ago that girls were taught that their roles in life were domestic—cooking, cleaning, birthing, and caring for a husband and children. Although this trend has changed in the past few decades, there are still many girls in the United States, not to mention other less gender-advanced countries, who are still being taught that their roles are restricted to the home.

That's not to say we haven't made progress. We clearly have. But as long as the binds that tie us to these roles linger in society, women will struggle.

LINGERING TIES THAT BIND US

In no realm have the historical ties that handcuff us to the past become more obvious than for women in public life. Secretary of State Hillary Clinton, First Lady Michelle Obama, former governor Sarah Palin, Supreme Court Justice Sonia Sotomayor, first female White House press secretary Dee Dee Myers—I could fill pages with names of high-profile women who have been held to a different standard, a much harsher standard than any man has endured, by a society that claims to believe in gender equality, yet clearly doesn't.

In her book *Why Women Should Rule the World*, Dee Dee Myers writes, "Women are caught in a double bind: expected to act like men—and punished for doing just that."[3] No one knows this better than Hillary Clinton. Her "So let's talk. Let's chat. Let's start a dialogue" video at the start of her candidacy was immediately criticized, not for one, but for two reasons. Some said she came across as too feminine, not strong enough to lead our country. Others criticized her for trying to create an image of being softer than she actually was. But the moment her language didn't comport with gender stereotypes, she was seen as too hard, too controlling, too impersonal. Even her tears were debated. Were they real or were they manipulatively manufactured? It's a perplexing and frustrating problem women in politics face each time they expose themselves to a public—of men and women alike—that criticizes them for being feminine (which is equated to being weaker) and criticizes them for trying to be more like men.

As Anne Kornblut writes in her book *Notes from the Cracked Ceiling*, "The dilemma over toughness vs. femininity has become a maddening but real dilemma for women in elections everywhere. . . . Clinton faced it from the moment her candidacy was merely rumored. It was the problem of the 'B-word'—the perception among women that she was, yes, tough, but to the point of being a bitch."[4]

And this kind of societal schizophrenia isn't unique to women who supposedly "expose" themselves by running for office (which is blaming the victim, if you ask me). Michelle Obama received a heavy dose of it during her husband's presidential campaign. A graduate of Princeton *and* Harvard, not only was she expected to take a backseat to her husband's political ambitions, she was criticized for being "too strong." How can a woman ever be "too strong"? It's a criticism a man would never face.

Unfortunately, examples of socially based double standards go on and on. Supreme Court Justice Sonia Sotomayor, who probably had one of the most consistent and unbiased records of any judge ever nominated for the Supreme Court, was characterized as temperamental, irrational, and domineering well before she ever made her "wise Latina" comment, which started its own gender-biased whirlwind. Yet male judges who actually are temperamental, irrational, and domineering, and who clearly use their experiences as men of various heritages to make their decisions (which there's nothing wrong with if their judgments are sound and follow the law) aren't subjected to anything close to the same scrutiny and criticism that Sotomayor was before her confirmation.

Dee Dee Myers discusses her experiences with double binds while working at the White House during President Bill Clinton's presidency. "As the first woman to serve as White House press secretary," she says in her book, "I definitely felt at times trapped by these competing expectations. I was supposed to be authoritative; after all, I was speaking for the President of the United States, The Most Powerful Man on Earth. But at the same time, I had to be likable—a quality that's a bonus, not a requirement, for men in the same position. If there's a way to do both, on many days, it eluded me."[5]

All these women's experiences highlight the point that societal binds are just as dangerous, if not more so, than workplace binds. Societal binds are powerful and can hit you from any direction—family members, friends, acquaintances, teachers, parents from your child's school, or the public at large. They're used by those "in power" to try to shape and influence the behavior of those who have less power. And in many cases, as we'll see through even more examples, they're very effective in doing just that.

But just as knowledge can effect change in the workplace, it can effect change in society, too. So it's important to recognize these double binds and the ways they can add stress to your life.

COMMON THEMES

Although the exact wording used to describe the societal double binds and stereotypes that women face may differ, they follow certain themes. There are more than I have included here, but the three themes I've chosen are the ones most likely to create stress in the lives of high-achieving women.

Leader/Head of the House/Breadwinner vs. Supporter

Regardless of the circumstances (in the home, at work, in the public eye), societal biases support the view that men are in charge. We see this theme play out constantly as society makes judgments about men and women in all aspects of their lives—public and private. No woman is safe from it. No woman escapes it. Men lead. Women follow. And although there are millions of men and women who don't agree with this outdated and faulty assumption, somehow their voices get shut out by the collective consciousness we call society.

Should we be surprised? Caroline Turner, a principal in the Athena Group and board member of the Women's Vision Foundation, says *no*. In her paper "Hillary Clinton and the Double Bind," Turner explains, "In the history of our culture there have been more men than women leaders; it is not surprising therefore, that the concept of 'leadership' brings to mind a predominantly masculine image."[6]

That's certainly true. All you have to do is look back through modern history to see examples of powerful men with their women behind them, supporting them through good and bad. Franklin had Eleanor. For Jack, there was Jackie. For Bill, there was Hillary. And for Barack, there is Michelle. And as we've seen recently, whenever women dare to step out of this "supporting" role that society has cast them to play, there's hell to pay.

We need look no further than Michelle Obama's experience to find evidence of this. "She's cold." "She's angry." "She's too strong." And *voilà*, we now have a warm, smiling, wonderfully supportive first lady planting vegetable gardens at the White House (which, of course, in classic double-bind style was even criticized).

Equally as bad, we have a media, fueled by society, that seems more interested in the clothes, shoes, hairstyle, and bare arms of the Princeton- and Harvard-educated woman than in her intellect, professional talents, and ambition. This is a perfect example of how powerful societal binds can be and how much they can affect women's lives. Although she wasn't elected to office, Michelle Obama is a bright, well-educated, and highly skilled first lady who serves as a powerful role model for girls and women, yet look at what she's being judged on.

Hillary Clinton is probably the most striking example of this leader/supporter bind. With an impressive résumé of her own, she struggled to be a first lady who was more than a supporter. But society would have none of it. After her husband's presidency, she fought hard to win a seat in Congress. She then took on the challenge of seeking the presidential nomination, and society went schizophrenic again. Every word she said was criticized. If she showed emotion, she was too weak to be a good leader. If she argued too much or too loudly, she was too strident, too bossy to be a good leader. It got to the point where it seemed that her advisers didn't even know what to advise.[7] Should she act like a woman or act like a man? No male candidate ever had to face such a double bind.

Yet, like Hillary, many women in prominent positions are confronted with this same bind. It doesn't matter what they do or say—they're damned if they do and damned if they don't. Turner explains how these gender-biased perceptions and the ensuing binds they create negatively impact all women leaders and those trying to become leaders. "The broad acceptance of an image of leadership that is skewed to the masculine end of this continuum gives rise to double binds: when women operate at the feminine end of the continuum, they are not seen as powerful, or as leaders at all. When women operate closer to the masculine end, however, this breaks cultural norms and makes men *and* women uncomfortable."[8]

"Uncomfortable" is an understatement.

Marriage/Family vs. Education/Career

Another common double bind faced by high-achieving women is the expectation that they will find both a meaningful and fulfilling career and a meaningful and fulfilling relationship—often at the same time. Although society seems to have accepted that women have the same freedom to pursue an education and a career as men do, that's fine, as long as we don't forget that there are other expectations as well, such as marriage and children.

"My dad teases me all the time," says Tonya, a twenty-nine-year-old forensic chemist. "He calls me an old maid. I know he's just kidding around, but I can tell a part of him isn't. I feel a lot of pressure over it. I'd really like to have a husband and a family. But finding the time seems impossible. It doesn't help either that all my friends from high school are already married. Some even have kids."

The fact is that many women find themselves caught in this bind. They would like to "have it all"—a college degree, an exciting career, a supportive husband, and a family. The problem is that it's extremely difficult to have it all. In fact, as workload and work hours in high-level positions have increased over the last few years, some women are finding that achieving "it all" is not even possible.

A survey of high-achieving women conducted by the National Parenting Association found that 40 percent of women between the ages of forty-one and fifty-five are not married. This is in contrast to 24 percent of unmarried men in this same age group.[9] Of course, not all women want to be married, and that brings on another double bind in and of itself. But for those who want to be married, it's not always easy to do. Aside from the internal pressure they feel to find a partner, there's the added pressure of the biological clock ticking away, not to mention the "old maid" stigma attached to unmarried women when they reach a certain age. For many, these kinds of pressures become a persistent source of stress in their lives. And even for those who do achieve some semblance of having "it all," it's not always as blissful as they might have expected.

Motherhood/Domesticity vs. Career

Motherhood versus career. It's the epic battle for women of the twentieth and twenty-first centuries. Just as with marriage, society is fine with women who want to pursue a career. But this doesn't relieve us of our societal "obligations" to take care of the home and to bear and raise children. There are obviously so many things wrong with these perceptions that it's hard to know where to begin, but let's start with taking care of the home and family.

Studies have shown that domestic responsibilities, such as taking care of their households and maintaining their relationships with family, children, and significant others, typically don't lessen for women who work outside the home. In fact, the National Parenting Association survey found that high-achieving working women are much more likely to assume primary responsibility for their homes and children than are their husbands or partners. The survey found that 50 percent of married, high-achieving women are primarily responsible for the preparation of meals (compared to only 9 percent of their husbands), and 51 percent take time off from work to care for a sick child (compared to only 9 percent of their husbands). Married, high-achieving career women also contribute an average of eleven hours a week to managing and executing household chores and responsibilities, which constitutes 61 percent of the total time spent on these weekly chores in their homes.[10] And when you're working sixty or seventy hours a week, which seems to be the norm for high-level executives, eleven hours of extra work time is hard to come by.

Another thorny dilemma women face under the scrutiny of societal biases relates to having children. Although women have the right to choose whether or not to have children, for most women who choose door number two, there's a backlash. The pressure comes from many sources—family, friends, and the constant influx of images of the millions of women who choose door number one.

Rather than seeing the choice to not have children as personal and private, society often views the decision as being inextricably linked to a woman's career, triggering a barrage of epithets such as "selfish," "power hungry," "greedy," and "self-centered." Even if you follow the "sticks and stones will break my bones, but words will never hurt me" philosophy of life, actions often do speak louder than words. There are the looks and gestures. The unintelligible whispers at weddings and family get-togethers. Your niece's school play where you're asked by the horde of proud, smiling moms about your children. But regardless of the source, the stress and the angst over the choice to not have children serve as a constant reminder that the path you've chosen goes against society's expectations.

You might think that choosing door number one would eliminate some of this pressure, but for many career-minded women, the stress remains—it's just different. Much of the stress exists because there simply are not enough hours in the day to devote to "getting a life" when work consumes the majority of that life. Most women who want children don't want to raise them alone. However, finding a partner and being able to devote enough time to make the partnership work can be difficult. And apart from artificial insemination (which some high-achieving women are choosing), it's difficult to have children without a partner. For many high-achieving women, this unfortunately equates to not always getting what they want.

The National Parenting Association survey found that although 86 percent of high-achieving women graduating from college reported that they *wanted* to have children, close to half of them turned out to be childless by age forty. Compare these figures to the 79 percent of men in the survey who indicated they wanted children and the 75 percent who later had children,[11] and it becomes rather obvious that while high-achieving men don't generally experience a gap between what they want and what they get (at least with respect to children), high-achieving women do. And with the incessant ticking of their biological clocks, knowing that with each tick their chances are less and less for conceiving, women can feel an enormous amount of stress added to their lives.

Of course, having children certainly doesn't remove stress; it often increases it. Juggling a career and children is one of the most difficult balancing acts a woman will ever perform. And as if that's not bad enough, society once again only makes it worse with the classic double bind of good moms/bad moms: good moms raise their children themselves; bad moms go to work and leave others to do it. This bind feeds directly into the guilt many working mothers feel about holding a job, regardless of whether that job is a financial necessity, a dream fulfilled, or both.

Remember the study that found that, compared to men, working women feel disproportionate stress related to their families' well-being while they're at work? The results found that women worry because they see a direct link between the time they spend at work and the negative effects on their families, such as their children eating more junk food, spending more time in front of the television, and just generally having less supervision.[12] But it doesn't stop there.

Working moms often find themselves in an impossible catch-22. Although they may enjoy the freedom and independence a job provides, they often feel guilty for leaving their children in the care of someone else during their workday. The same guilt is often experienced by former stay-at-home moms who find themselves back in the workforce, not by choice but because their partner was laid off or because their family needs a second income. And, of course, single moms usually have no choice at all in the matter. Although they may enjoy what they do, they often have to work just to survive and support their family.

At the crux of the stress these working women experience is an underlying question that has sparked a highly charged and ongoing social debate: Do children raised by stay-at-home moms "do better" than children who receive some form of childcare while their moms work?

The first problem is the flaw in the question. Do better at what? Do children in childcare do better with sharing? Do they do better academically? But setting this fundamental flaw aside for a moment, many working moms worry, mostly because of inaccurate assumptions they glean from untested societal biases that suggest that their children are at a disadvantage by being in childcare.

Well, I'm happy to report that at least on that front, there is good news. The results of a study fifteen years in the making suggest that all that worry and stress over children in childcare is for naught. The study, conducted by the National Institute of Child Health and Human Development (NICHD), followed more than one thousand American children over a fifteen-year period, beginning at one month of age.[13] The results surprised many.

Children who experienced 100 percent maternal care (no outside childcare) didn't actually fare any better than children who received nonmaternal care, including all forms of care—center-based childcare, family-based childcare, relatives, and babysitters. This held true even for those children who started daycare as infants (before twelve months of age). In fact, children who spent time in high-quality childcare showed higher cognitive and language skills and better school readiness scores than other children, including those with stay-at-home mothers.

The one negative to come out of the study was that a small percentage of the children who spent long hours in childcare centers had more behavioral problems, such as fighting and temper tantrums. However, researchers considered these problems to be normal, not severe, and temporary, usually disappearing between third and fifth grade. The other not-so-good news, not surprisingly, is that children in childcare settings are more likely to get ear infections and upper respiratory infections, and to experience stomach problems. But as a whole, the results are good news for working mothers who are stressing out over leaving their children with someone else while they work.

Also important for stressed-out working moms to know is that family features, such as parents' educational levels, family income, a two-parent home environment, the mother's sensitivity and psychological adjustment, and the social and cognitive quality of the home environment, are more strongly and more consistently associated with children's development than whether or not their children are in childcare. Another interesting finding was that stay-at-home mothers don't actually spend that many additional hours with their children. Yes, they are with their children in the same house for more hours, but their social interactions with them are only about 20 percent more than those of mothers who work outside of the home.

Finally, at least one study has found that today's mothers, in many instances, are spending a greater number of hours in child-centered activities than mothers of the 1960s, which surprised many, since mothers of that era are usually thought of as being more family-oriented than mothers of today. The study found that "mothers' time caring for children is at least as high, perhaps higher, than it was at the height of the baby boom in 1965," leading researchers to conclude that "children, on average, are increasingly advantaged in terms of the parental time and attention they receive."[14]

These findings are good news for guilt-ridden working mothers. There is no scientific data that shows that being in childcare versus being at home is detrimental or harmful to children. On the other hand, a mother's behavior and emotional state do actually affect children's healthy development, as does the amount of *quality* time spent with children. So, working moms, stop stressing over the good mom/bad mom bind. The truth is that it's not real. Quality is more important than quantity, and the guilt (i.e., stress) you feel about working is likely to have more negative effects on you and your children than working itself.

ADDED BURDENS, ADDED STRESS

The societal double binds described in this chapter represent added burdens that are unique to women, burdens that create additional stress in lives that are already brimming with it. As women, we live in a world that sends us conflicting messages: on the one hand, society tells us that if we work hard, we can take the checkered flag and win the race; yet the other hand is weighing down the car so much that we have to struggle to get there. In doing my research for this book, I came across an editorial piece written by Dan Antony for the *University Register*, the newspaper of the University of Minnesota, which nicely sums up many of the points we've discussed.

Antony writes,

> Looking around, it's easy to see how many opportunities that women in modern society have that were not open to them in any practical sense previously. But digging beneath the surface shows how little the position of women has changed. The key is to understand that these are additional opportunities. Very few of the expectations laid on women before have changed. My sisters received a lot of encouragement (and pressure) to succeed and get an education (as did I), a modern egalitarian vision. Less egalitarian was the pressure applied for them to get married and have kids. Parents eager for grandchildren aren't particularly sympathetic to the plight of the modern woman. . . . Society allows women to explore new roles, but only if they continue to fill the old ones as well. Society hasn't changed the roles of women, they've added to them, creating an extra burden for modern women.[15]

While this is true, it doesn't mean that you have to accept it. Author and civil rights leader James Brown once said, "Not everything that is faced can be changed, but nothing can be changed until it is faced."[16] You can give in to the power of these double binds and let them influence the outcome of your race, or you can take their power away by calling attention to them whenever they happen, as we discussed earlier. In a world where half of the population is female, I'm hopeful that our collective voices will eventually be able to defuse and end these harmful and unfair double binds. Until that time, it's important for you to use your own unique voice in ways that will promote positive change and reduce the stress you experience in the areas of your life where these impossible binds still exist.

Chapter 4

BELLS AND WHISTLES:
Technological Stressors That
Lead to Burnout[1]

*Bells and Whistles: innovative and flashy,
but often unnecessary features of a product.*
—from Answers.com

We certainly have our work cut out for us—workplace stress, double binds, stereotypes. It's easy to see why it's so hard to get our jobs done with all the stressful distractions going on around us. I wish I could say that this chapter was going to lighten the load. After all, it's about all the bells and whistles we buy for ourselves, all those gadgets that are supposed to make our lives easier. But I can't lie to you. Your life has pretty much gone to the dogs when it comes to technology. You, my friend, have become conditioned.

Much like the dog in Ivan Pavlov's quintessential classical conditioning experiment that was trained to salivate by the pairing of food with the ringing of a bell, we humans have become hopelessly conditioned to our own bells. Every time we hear one, in all the forms they come in today—beeps, swooshes, dings, vibrations, or any of the other millions of tones we proudly program into our electronic devices—we salivate.

There's a difference, though, between us and the dog. Unlike the poor dog, we're not helpless animals at the mercy of a researcher. We're active and eager participants in the passionate connection we've developed with being connected. But that isn't necessarily good.

HOPELESSLY ADDICTED

In today's constantly connected world, it's truly rare to find anyone who isn't using a cell phone, personal computer, e-mail, or instant messaging—in

73

some cases, all at the same time. In fact, the tasty morsels (a.k.a. reinforcement) we get when we use these devices have become so important to us that we program our gadgets to alert us the moment someone decides to reach out and touch us. The sad truth is that we've become hopelessly addicted to instant communication.

A major part of that addiction is the instant gratification we receive when we're able to connect with just about anyone at just about any time, any place, anywhere. Feeding that dependency even further are the instant answers, instant money, instant data, instant everything we get when all is well in the world of connectivity. Need cash for the newest gadget that just went on sale at Best Buy? No worries. Just hit the ATM. Can't sleep until you find out the latest financial news in the Japanese market? No worries. Just jump out of bed and log on to Nikkei.com. Want to play chess with someone in Africa? There's an app for that.

Let's face it. We've become a society of instant-gratification junkies. Don't believe me? Just think back to the last time an electronic device went down in your life . . . anywhere—at home, at work, at the phone company, the bank, the post office, the mall, you name it. Remember that initial sense of panic? Whatever you were trying to do—make a purchase, download a picture, e-mail a long-lost friend—just stopped. As the minutes ticked by and no lives were lost, the panic likely evolved into frustration, stress, and maybe even a little rage. Why? Because, as addicts, losing our connections thrusts us into a state of withdrawal until the system goes back up and we can get our fix.

The same kind of thing happens when someone loses a cell phone. Panic quickly sets in. What calls am I missing? Who is trying to reach me? I've known people who became so distressed over being separated from their phones that they actually went out and bought a new one within an hour of losing theirs. Now that's addiction with a capital *A*.

And although not everyone is that addicted to technology, there are few who can claim little or no dependence on what some are aptly calling "weapons of mass communication."[2] The role these devices play in the daily battles we wage with stress have yet to be fully realized. But one thing is for certain: while they have improved our lives in many ways, including increasing our opportunities for flexibility in the workplace, they have created stressors that were not present years ago.

BLURRED BOUNDARIES

Cell phones, laptops, desktops, pagers, text messages, instant messages, fax machines, and e-mails badly blur the boundaries between work and home. For some, a boundary doesn't even exist. "I gave up that delusion a long time ago," said Alexia, a criminal defense lawyer who works as a sole practitioner. "I'm constantly juggling deadlines, trial dates, jail visits. Throw in a few emergency hearings, calls from family members in the middle of the night, telling me their child, husband, mother, you name it, has been arrested. For me, my work hours are when I'm awake and my off time is when I'm asleep, and there's certainly not much of that going on."

But even in cases that are not as extreme as Alexia's, the blurring of boundaries leaves little time free from interruptions. It wasn't all that long ago that lunch hours gave us a double dose of protection from stress. The lunch itself provided the calories we needed to sustain our energy through the rest of the workday, and the *act* of going to lunch, just getting out of the office, offered a break from the workday. However, in today's world, it's rare to experience a lunch that isn't interrupted by texts or phone calls—if you're even lucky enough to get out to lunch.

Chance meetings with colleagues in the hallway are another example of an opportunity for respite that is quickly going the way of the dodo. These meetings, even if the conversation is about work, give us a chance to socially connect with something other than a lighted screen. They give us opportunities to exchange information with a real human being or a chance to just talk casually with a coworker. But in today's work world, these "mini-breaks" are getting fierce competition from the dings, beeps, and vibrations that pull us away from the social world and back into the virtual world.

Even business travel, something that once allowed for at least a little downtime between point A and point B, has been hijacked. There isn't a major airport in the country where you can't log in. And more recently, the airline industry itself succumbed to the pressure, spending millions of dollars just to offer travelers the luxury of connecting in the air (as if we need more connection time).

But that's not all. Propelled by increasingly advanced technology, globalization has not only made the world a much smaller place, it's made us interdependent.[3] Many companies today are internationally based or are outsourcing work to other countries to lower their costs. As a result, an employee in Houston may need to wait for a decision from upper management in London before she can move forward on a project, or employees working on a deadline in India may need input from a worker in California. That's what technology gives us—the ability to connect to anyone, anytime, anywhere in the world, in many cases, instantly.

Yet while a smaller world may be an advantage to businesses, for individuals working across several time zones, the costs can be steep. Not only can it wreak havoc on your sleep cycle, it can also destroy any illusions you may have of maintaining boundaries between work and life. In some cases, it literally makes the workday endless.

DECREASED PRODUCTIVITY

So we're a bit addicted. And we're developing boundary issues. Is that all bad news? So what if technology has added a little more stress to our lives? Just look at how much more versatile and productive we've become. Okay . . . let's look.

As a psychologist, whenever I want answers to perplexing or controversial questions, I've been trained to look at the data—the evidence that is generated from scientific studies. People can say and think a lot of things, but only the evidence tells us the real story. And in the case of *The People v. Technology*, it turns out that we, "The People," are getting our butts kicked.

Researchers have found that we "users" (that's the nice term researchers use for instant communication addicts) believe we have control over when we choose to respond to an "alert"—that beep, ding, or vibration signaling that a message is waiting. Therefore, we see no need to disable these alerts. But the truth is that we don't have as much control as we think we have.[4] Often, the identity of the "sender"—the intruder trying to access us while we're working—and the content of the message influence whether we respond, even if the alert comes in when we're working on something important. In other words, we may have the best intentions of not letting anything distract us from our work, but good intentions often fall to the wayside depending on who's at the other end of the communication and how interesting the communication is to us.

But what does this do to our productivity? Quite a lot, as it turns out, and not in the way many people think. Once we divert our attention from what we're doing by responding to an alert, we rarely leave what we were working on in a manner that will enable us to easily resume it (e.g., not saving the document, not marking our place, not completing a sentence before we break away). And although we like to think we're in control of how much time we spend away from a task when we switch from one to another, we're not. It turns out that we're largely unaware of how much time we spend away from the project we were originally working on. Not only that, when we break away from a project to respond to an alert, we're often drawn to other tasks or alerts, unrelated to the initial alert or to what we were originally working on.[5]

And it just goes downhill from there. When we finally return to the original task, it takes us quite a bit of time to mentally return to where we left off. In fact, researchers Shamsi Iqbal at the University of Illinois and Eric Horvitz of Microsoft Research have found that when we leave a task to respond to an e-mail and then return to the task, it takes us, on average, about sixteen minutes to get back to the point of productivity we were at before we were distracted. For instant messages (IMs), the average time to get back to where we were is eleven to twelve minutes.[6]

I'll let you do the math. How many times a day do you allow yourself to get distracted by an IM? Now multiply that by twelve minutes, then add the amount of time you spend responding to each IM. Next, figure out how many times a day you allow yourself to get distracted by an e-mail. Multiply that by sixteen, and then add. . . . I think you get the picture.

Productivity suffers when we allow ourselves to become distracted by all the bells and whistles that have become a constant in our lives. And when productivity suffers, our workloads increase, and therefore our stress levels increase. The verdict is in. The People lose.

CHANGES IN WORK PATTERNS

Not only do interruptions decrease productivity, they also cause changes in our work patterns. Researcher Gloria Mark and her colleagues have found that any type of disruption, whether it be related to what we're working on (a question about a tax code while we're working on a related tax form) or unrelated (a phone call about a purchase while we're preparing a quote for a new client), causes a change in our work patterns.[7]

One of the most obvious changes is the change in our work rhythm. A disruption pulls us off-course, and in doing so, puts us off of our pace. There are other negative consequences as well. Mark and her colleagues discovered that interruptions cause us to work faster to compensate for lost time, which cascades into other problems. For example, the more interruptions we experience, the bigger our workload becomes. This, in turn, causes us to feel more time pressure and requires more effort to get the work out in time.

AHHH . . .

"Take a deep breath." We hear that all the time when we're stressed, right? The assumption, of course, is that you're going to let it out. What good is a deep breath if there isn't the *ahhh* at the end? But according to Linda Stone—a former executive at Apple and Microsoft and currently a writer, speaker, and consultant on consumer trends—technology is literally taking away our *ahhhs*.

Stone says that one of the most significant changes to our lives in the last twenty years is "screen time," meaning the time we spend in front of a television, video game, computer, or mobile device.[8] As you might expect, our screen time these days is pretty substantial. The latest research indicates that although the types of screens people gravitate toward vary greatly depending on age, the total amount of time people spend in front of a screen averages about eight and a half hours a day.[9] And that's where the trouble starts.

According to Stone, being in front of one of these screens causes many of us to experience "e-mail apnea," a term she coined to describe the temporary cessation of breathing or the shallow breathing that occurs in anticipation of what we'll discover in all those e-mails and texts and IMs just waiting to be opened.[10] Apparently, it's so stimulating that it takes our breath away—but not in a good way.

Shallow breathing and forgetting to exhale have long been associated with increased stress and stress-related conditions. When we hold our breath, it throws our biochemistry off, which impacts us not only physically but mentally as well. Our blood pressure rises, our heart rate increases, and the amount of carbon dioxide in our body increases. More important, not enough oxygen gets to our cells, tissues, and organs—including our brain.

While this may not seem like such a big deal, it actually is. Oxygen isn't just important to our bodies, it's vital. As we've seen from natural disasters around the world, people can go weeks without food and days without water, but we can't survive for even a few minutes without oxygen. Simply put, when we don't breathe right, we're stressing out our bodies.

FAMILY AND SOCIAL CONNECTIONS

Technology can also have a negative impact on our relationships. Sandra was willing to overlook her husband texting at the movie theater. She was even willing to overlook the phone calls he frequently took during dinner. But the frantic drive around Paris while they were on their dream vacation so he could find a place to "plug in" was the final straw.

"His job is very demanding," she said, flustered. "He says that's the reason he needs to be on 24/7, but the truth is he's completely addicted. I really think he needs 'it' as much as 'it' needs him."

Stories like Sandra's are becoming more and more common in marriage counseling sessions. Because of the pull of technology, many partners report feeling isolated, as if their partner is present in body but missing in mind much of the time. And these feelings aren't isolated to partners. When we're glued to a screen as much as we are, it's not surprising to see the "here in body, there in mind" experience playing out in our relationships with friends, extended family, and children.

The experience falls right in line with the ongoing debate over the social impact of technology. At the crux of the argument is whether technology is causing us to sacrifice social connections for digital and virtual ones. In 2006, this debate was further fueled by the release of a study by sociologists Miller McPherson, Lynn Smith-Lovin, and Matthew Brashears. The study found that since 1985, Americans have become much more socially isolated and have fewer connections with their neighbors and communities, which led the researchers to speculate that one cause for this might be the dramatic rise in Internet usage and mobile devices over the last twenty years.[11]

These findings spurred the Pew Research Center—a nonprofit organization that investigates trends, issues, and attitudes affecting families and communities—to conduct a nationwide survey to explore the relationship between technology and social connections. Their results found that, although it's true that our social networks have shrunk by about one-third since 1985, face-to-face contact is still the most common method of connecting with family and friends. The data showed that in a typical year, face-to-face contacts occurred an average of 210 days, compared to 195 days of mobile phone contact, 125 days of text messaging, 72 days of e-mail contact, and 55 days of instant messaging. The survey also found that Internet usage doesn't pull us away from public places. We still go to parks, cafés, and restaurants; the difference is that now we go with our devices.[12]

But is this good news? Not if you consider it from Linda Stone's perspective. Stone, who, as we just learned, came up with the term "e-mail apnea," has noted something else of significance—something she calls continuous partial attention.[13]

According to Stone, continuous partial attention (CPA) is a mechanism we use to keep from missing anything in a world in which we're constantly bombarded with data and alerts that prevent us from focusing on any one thing, including people. In contrast to multitasking, where the underlying motivation is to be more productive and more efficient by pairing a mundane activity with an activity that requires thought (e.g., writing a letter while eating lunch, taking a phone call while filling out routine paperwork), the underlying motivation of CPA is to scan all incoming material to make sure we don't miss anything important. The problem with this, however, is that to keep from missing something, we have to engage in two (or more) activities that require concentration and thought (e.g., having a conversation while reading an e-mail, talking on the phone while driving). Not an easy thing to do, or, at least, not an easy thing to do well.

When we're in CPA mode, nothing receives our full attention. This may explain why so many people experience a disconnect with family and friends. Even though they may physically be in the same room, mentally they're far, far away. And that's not a good thing for our stress levels, first, because it can cause tension in our relationships, and second, because it can make us feel like we always have to be on high alert.

ALWAYS ON

Perhaps the most problematic of all the stressors created by technology are the expectations created by it. Because most people are always connected in some way or another, we are at the point where others expect it—all the time. As Amanda, a corporate attorney in a large Miami law firm, describes it: "My firm represents clients all over the world, wealthy clients who pay us a lot of money to be available to them whenever legal questions come up. Most of the calls only last a few minutes, but I am literally on call 24/7."

Of course, the problem is that although one call may take only a few minutes, busy professionals sometimes receive hundreds of different forms of contact each day, ranging from phone calls to text messages to e-mails. Not only does it take time to respond to all these alerts, but their random arrival at all times of the day and night wreaks havoc on our ability to predict what our workload is going to be on any given day. It's hard to prepare for something you can't predict.

But the expectations of others and the unpredictability are only part of the problem. The other part is the expectations we place on ourselves. Carmen, a business owner of two successful online wholesale companies, is a perfect example: "I have this unwritten rule. I don't even know where it came from, but if I don't get back to someone's e-mail or phone call within an hour, I feel like I'm not doing my job, like I'm not meeting my clients' expectations." And she's not alone.

In *Seduction and Risk: The Emergence of Extreme Jobs*, economist Sylvia Ann Hewlett and her colleagues found that 61 percent of respondents to her survey on extreme jobs believe that being readily accessible and available is a critical component of being successful at their jobs.[14] Laudable? Maybe. But this kind of availability in a world that doesn't sleep comes at a heavy price.

INCREASED STRESS

The price is increased stress in lives that are already overstressed to begin with. In fact, in each of the areas previously described, the resulting consequence is added stress in all areas of our lives—psychological, physical, social, family, and work.

- Blurred boundaries increase our stress levels by expanding the workday to hours never before seen in modern history, resulting in loss of sleep and the feeling of needing to always be on high alert. We never know when a crisis will erupt and drag us back into the fray.

- Technology's role in decreased productivity and changes in our work patterns increase stress by making it seem that no matter how long or hard or fast we work, the work never seems to end and the pile never seems to diminish.
- Technology impacts our physical well-being by affecting our breathing, blood pressure, and heart rate.
- When devices pull us away from social connections, we potentially lose a source of support, which has been found to serve as a buffer between us and our stressors.
- When we don't pay attention to our relationships because we're busy with our devices, we can create tension in our families, increase fighting, and add to our risk for divorce—all of which obviously increase stress.
- When our devices cause us to engage in continuous partial attention, they put us in a state of high alert, which makes our bodies and minds think we're in a state of crisis, taxing us both physically and mentally.
- And finally, when we're always on, there is no opportunity to replenish our reserves.

But I did say there was good news. . . .

MAYBE NOT HOPELESS

The good news is that you're not a dog, and I say that with all seriousness. As I said at the beginning of this chapter, Pavlov's dog was at the mercy of Pavlov. But you're not a dog and you're not at anyone's mercy. Or at least you don't have to be. Here are some ways to overcome your addiction to technology so you can get back to living in the real world.

Taking Control of Your Breathing

Let's start with the easiest thing first—breathing. I know! It's not new or exciting. In fact, it's one of the oldest and most basic stress reducers around. And yes, high-achieving women often want something exciting as an anti-dote. But correct breathing can be your secret weapon. It happens to be one of the most effective and powerful techniques to reduce tension—even for the most driven of us. Surprisingly, though, few of us use it to our advantage.

Why? Mainly because breathing is something we do 24/7—while we're awake and while we're asleep. It just happens, so we take it for granted. But if you train yourself to take advantage of what it has to offer, you should notice results right away.

One of the things that makes breathing such a powerful stress reducer is that when it's done correctly, it's fail-proof. It would take a concerted effort on your part to remain tense when you're taking deep breaths. Some even say it can't be done (but I try not to tell high-achieving women something can't be done—they tend to take it as a challenge, and we don't need to go there).

It also doesn't hurt that it's free, but even better is the fact that it doesn't take any additional time out of your over-burdened schedule. You don't have to take any special classes or attend any workshops on breathing (although they certainly are offered). You just need to learn how to do it right, and that's easy.

Now, you're probably asking, if it's so easy and so good for you, why isn't everyone doing it? The answer is that, while it may be easy, it isn't automatic. When you use breathing to reduce stress, there are two challenges to overcome.

The first challenge is training yourself to breathe correctly. We all breathe, but we all don't breathe correctly. And the more stress you're under, the more likely it is that you aren't breathing correctly.

When people feel stressed or anxious, they tend to take short, shallow breaths. This increases your heart rate, raises your blood pressure, increases carbon dioxide levels, and lowers oxygen levels. When your muscles and brain cells are receiving insufficient oxygen, you can experience muscle tension and headaches. In fact, as Dr. Marcelle Pick, cofounder of the Women to Women Clinic in Yarmouth, Maine, points out, shallow breathing over time can cause actual changes in our lungs, which decreases the amount of oxygen available to our tissues.[15] Fortunately, these changes can be corrected by proper breathing.

To breathe properly, pull in air slowly through your nose. Don't let it stop in your chest. Pull it all the way down through your abdomen, then let the air out slowly through your mouth. By doing this, you're expanding your lung capacity and fully oxygenating your blood, which then carries that oxygen to your muscles and tissues. The end result is that muscle tension is reduced and you should feel an overall sense of well-being.

An easy way to check if you're breathing correctly is by placing one hand on your chest and one hand on your abdomen. You should feel the air moving through your chest and down into your abdomen. If the hand on your chest rises higher than the hand on your abdomen, you're keeping too much air in your chest. Just pull the air deeper down into your lungs on the next breath until you get a rhythm going. It's that easy!

But as I said, there's a second challenge. You have to train yourself to monitor your breathing. Right now, you're probably very focused on your breathing and it seems easy enough, but that's only because you're focusing on it. You'll be surprised how easily you fall back into your old breathing patterns as soon as we move on to another topic. So the key to overcoming this challenge is to develop a *habit* of good breathing, and that's going to take practice.

Practice breathing? Yes. Breathing is automatic. Good breathing is not— at least not yet. To make good breathing automatic, you need to condition yourself to pay attention to your breathing throughout the day just as you've conditioned yourself to pay attention to the beeps and the dings you receive throughout the day. In fact, you can actually use your technology to your advantage when it comes to practicing your breathing.

Most computers and mobile devices have built-in reminders that you can program to intermittently remind you throughout the day to breathe correctly. Digital Post-its, e-mail reminders, pop-ups, bells, whistles—use whatever program works best for you. But if you're going to use a tone, I'd recommend using one that is distinct from the tones you've already programmed, like your ringtone or message alert. We're not trying to add to the burden of your life through devices. This is a beneficial service your devices can provide you in your battle against stress.

Once you select your reminder of choice, program it to intermittently remind you to check your breathing throughout the day. You can set the frequency to whatever you feel most comfortable with, but like anything else, the more you practice, the sooner it will become habit. You may also want to try good old-fashioned reminders. Since you'll be breathing everywhere you go, the strategic placement of sticky notes in your car, on your refrigerator, in the bathroom, or on your desk can go a long way in speeding up your mastery of proper breathing.

The concept is simple. As soon as you receive the "reminder," whether it be digital or nontechnical, focus on your breathing just like you're doing now. Once you get the hang of it, it shouldn't be too distracting because, after all, it's just breathing. Try not to get frustrated if you revert to your old ways within minutes after each reminder (because obviously that would defeat the purpose). Over time, as your brain becomes trained to breathe correctly, you won't need as many reminders to pay attention to it. You'll just automatically do it.

And while we're on the subject of paying attention, you also should train yourself to pay attention to your body throughout the day. Just as your body tells you when there is pain, your body also tells you when there is stress. You've likely trained yourself to ignore these signals. But just like anything else, you can untrain yourself with practice. Paying attention to your body (and your breathing) is especially important right after high-pressured situations. It's hard to do when you're in the middle of a crisis (although it can be done with practice), but if you can train yourself to pay attention to what's happening with your body immediately following a stressful event, you'll be miles ahead of everyone else. In fact, tension and breathing go hand in hand. As soon as you feel your muscles are tense and your stomach is knotted, focus on your breathing, and the tension should go away fairly quickly.

Teaching yourself to breathe correctly is obviously not going to remove all your stress. Nothing will. A stress-free life is not possible, especially for you. However, if correct breathing is done, it can go a long way in reducing the tension you feel, and a reduction in tension is a reduction in stress.

Getting Control of Your Devices

Here's where it gets a little harder. Okay, probably a lot harder. It's pretty clear that with few exceptions we've become a world of technology junkies who'll do just about anything to get our instant communication fixes. So you'll probably find that controlling your breathing is a piece of cake compared to controlling your devices. But it can be done. All it takes is discipline and the ability to forgive yourself when you fall off the wagon, which is probably going to happen a lot at first. So take a deep breath, don't forget the *ahhh*, and let's get started.

(1) Because interruptions can be so disruptive to productivity and performance, if possible, turn off the dings, dongs, beeps, and bells when you're

working on a specific task or project. Unfortunately, due to the nature of addiction, I've come to learn that I need to define what "if possible" means, or, more important, what it doesn't mean. "If possible" does *not* mean if it doesn't make you uncomfortable or anxious. If you're addicted, turning off your alerts *will definitely* make you uncomfortable and anxious. Just breathe deeply and think of the discomfort as a necessary part of the recovery process. "If possible" actually means if responding isn't a part of your job description. If it is, forget #1 and go to #2.

(2) If you can't disable your alerts, try speaking to the powers that be about their expectations of how quickly you're expected to respond to alerts. It might be a good idea to have your boss read this chapter before you ask. I doubt if most employers realize how much time their employees are losing by all the disruptions. If that doesn't work and you find out you're expected to respond within a certain time period, set a schedule where you check your e-mail or phone messages every half-hour, hour, or whatever the time period is, and prioritize, which means handle only what is critical as quickly as possible. Then return to whatever you were working on.

(3) Instant messages are often used when a response is needed immediately, but this isn't always the case. Sometimes, it's the addict on the other end who just needs a fix of instant communication. If you find yourself on the receiving end of such a communication, quickly inform your fellow addict that you're in recovery—in other words, you're working—and can't respond. Then turn your IM status to "invisible," which you should've done before you started your project anyway. Keep your status on invisible until you've finished the task, and then once you clock out, you can reward yourself for a job well done by IMing until your heart is content (or until someone in your life rips the device out of your hands).

(4) If possible (see #1 for definition), leave a message on your cell phone telling callers that you respond to messages only between the hours of (fill in the blank). Then, follow your own instructions and return messages only during that specific period of time. This accomplishes two things: (1) it removes any expectation on the part of the caller that you'll respond immediately or even quickly, and (2) you're now in better control of your schedule. When someone calls you, it's usually because that's the best time for *them* to talk. That doesn't necessarily coincide with the best time in your schedule for *you* to talk. If you have to leave a message when you return the call, so be it. Just think of it as giving yourself more time to return your other calls.

(5) Better yet, if someone else answers your calls, tell them to encourage callers to e-mail their message to you as opposed leaving a phone message. If you answer your own calls, leave your e-mail address on your voice mail and encourage callers to send an e-mail. Most people will talk more than they are willing to write, so having them send an e-mail is likely to cut down on the time spent listening to what they have to tell you. You can also decide on a convenient time to review the e-mails, and you don't have to worry about forgetting what someone told you when they called. But be careful not to let this backfire by reading and responding to e-mails during work-free times at home or throughout your workday to the point that it interrupts or interferes with your other work.

(6) If possible, set aside a specific amount of time each day to respond to e-mails (or several periods of time each day, if you get an exceedingly large number of e-mails). During that time, clean out your in-box as much as you can by (a) quickly deleting spam or messages that don't require a response, (b) not being shy about using the forward feature; if the message is more appropriate for someone else to handle, send it on its merry way so you can move on to the messages that require your response, and (c) respond to the messages that require your response. The ultimate goal (and challenge) is to have an empty in-box at the end of your allotted e-mail time.[16]

Although it may take you some time to untrain yourself from responding to all the bells and whistles you've brought into your life, none of these strategies actually add anything else to your plate. In fact, by controlling these devices rather than letting them control you, you will have more time on your hands—try to resist filling it up with work.

Chapter 5

DRIVING TOO FAST FOR CONDITIONS:
Individual Stressors That Lead to Burnout

Driving Too Fast for Conditions: driving at a speed that impairs one's ability to negotiate curves or maneuver around obstacles in the roadway.
—from USLegal.com

So you have a good sense of the road conditions you're up against. The crowd is still roaring, but at least you know what you're facing, and the bells and whistles are in check, so they won't distract you. But none of these things are going to help you if you're moving so fast that you're going to crash and burn before you get to the finish line. When you're in the driver's seat, it's sometimes hard to know how fast you're going without a gauge to tell you.

Think of a road trip. Once you get going, it's easy to lose track of how fast you're traveling because after a while, it feels like you're going slowly. So you go a little faster and a little faster until the car starts giving you signals that you're moving a little too fast. The engine gets louder. The steering wheel starts to shake. These warning signs are cues that you need to slow down . . . except when you're driving a car with a high-performance engine.

In high-performance cars, 100 mph can seem pretty slow, and your engine is so powerful that it's not giving you any warning signs. So you just keep racing along at dangerously high speeds until you come up on a big curve or run into a major obstacle, and that's when you start spinning out of control.

The same thing happens to high-achieving women. You live inside your own mental high-performance car, so to you the speed seems perfectly normal. Everyone else is amazed. "How does she do that? How can she keep everything together when she's flying along at that rate of speed?" But to you, zipping around the track at 200 mph is just what you do. It's who you are, so it seems normal.

And if the road conditions were perfect, if there were no obstacles, no dangerous curves, and if you refueled every now and then, you could probably keep speeding along forever. But the roads you're traveling on are definitely not obstacle-free. There is debris everywhere, flying in from every direction, causing dings, dents, scratches, fuel leaks, and wear and tear on your tires. Combine this with the type of person you are and before you know it, you're driving too fast for the road conditions—and that can be dangerous. That's why it's important to understand the factors that you, as a high-achieving woman, bring to the race, the qualities that make you who you are. When you understand this, you can figure out which gauges you can tweak inside the car to help control your speed.

WHAT MAKES HIGH-ACHIEVING WOMEN HIGH ACHIEVERS?

Many of the high-achieving women I know don't necessarily think of themselves as high achievers, although they know they're different. "I'm a teacher," said Vicky, a community college instructor. "I'm passionate about what I do and I usually go above and beyond the call of duty, but I don't think that qualifies me as a high achiever."

I hear comments like this more than you can imagine. But it's not status or job title that makes high-achieving women high achievers. It's how their minds work.

Dr. Harriet Braiker, a clinical psychologist and management consultant, offers insight into the psychological mind-sets of high-achieving women in her book *The Type E* Woman*. She writes, "I define the term, 'high-achieving' as a psychological state rather than as a sociological status. In other words, the term refers to a way of thinking more than to a specific level of achievement per se."[1]

So, it's not what you do for a living that defines you as a high-achieving woman, it's your state of mind, how you psychologically respond to challenges, which then propels you toward excellence in achievement. In order to understand what drives you (unfortunately sometimes into a wall), you first must understand the psychology behind who you are.

THE PSYCHOLOGY OF HIGH-ACHIEVING WOMEN

To understand the psychology of high-achieving women, you first have to know a little bit about personality styles. Personality styles are the filters through which we view our experiences. These filters influence how we think and feel about our experiences and how we react to them.

Within each personality style is a variety of traits or tendencies that characterizes that particular style. For instance, extroverts tend to be outgoing, gregarious, and comfortable in groups. Introverts tend to be the opposite. However, personality styles and the traits associated with them are not all-or-none. They, like communication styles, exist along a continuum.

Some extroverts are extremely outgoing; others, only a little. Neither quality is right or wrong—just different. Also, whether or not a trait or quality is displayed can be affected by circumstances. Although extroverts are *usually* friendly, if they're angry with someone, they may not be. Introverts are *usually* uncomfortable in groups, but in a small group of close friends, they may be very comfortable. The point here is that the style, traits, and qualities of a person aren't set in stone. Although it's easier to do the things we're more inclined to do, we can also do things we're not inclined to do, especially if it's important to us or if a specific situation calls for it.

Qualities of High-Achieving Women: The Good and the Bad

If you haven't figured it out yet, as a high-achieving woman, you possess some rather unique qualities. If you're like most, you enjoy having multiple pots on the fire at all times, and you grow easily bored during those rare instances when your jam-packed life slows down. Not only do you usually get the job done faster and better than anyone else, you often do the work of two people. If there is a new frontier to conquer, you want to conquer it. If there is a problem to solve, you want to solve it. You work hard to get where you want to be, and even after you arrive, you keep looking for new challenges that will keep your engine racing. This all happens because high achievers are motivated by achievement. You're internally driven to strive for excellence.

Of course, these are all good qualities to have. Excellent qualities, in fact. These are the things that make you different, that make you stand out from the rest of the crowd. Unfortunately, the same traits that cause you to get ahead can also cause you to crash. Why? Because these qualities make your engine run faster. They push you to jump into the race rather than sit on the sidelines and let all the excitement rush by. They draw you into situations that present challenges and test your abilities and your stamina. But at the same time, all these things, by their very nature, increase stress. And this is particularly true if these traits happen to be at the extreme end of their respective continuums (e.g., the extreme end of the "striving for excellence" continuum is perfectionism).

Consider the trait of perseverance. On one end of the continuum is indifference and apathy; at the other end is rigid, unbending diligence. People who are indifferent aren't likely to seek out or engage in behaviors that will lead to stress, whereas people who are diligent will. So, forgetting about all the external stressors we discussed earlier, the mere fact that you're a high-achieving woman makes it more likely you'll have more stress in your life than those who are not.

Now, stress isn't all bad. Some stress is good. Stress can motivate us (like when we need to help someone in a life-threatening situation), stress can make us more careful when we're in dangerous situations (like when we're crossing a busy street), and stress can help us focus (like when we're taking a test). As a high-achieving woman, your goal is not to eliminate the stress caused by your personality traits, because some of that stress is good stress. It helps you do what you need to do. Your aim is to identify ways in which those traits may be causing *bad stress* in your life so you can gain better control over it.

Striving for Excellence

Striving for excellence is one of the hallmark characteristics of high achievers. You don't only want to get the job done, you want to get it done as well as it can possibly be done, better than it's ever been done before. You go beyond the call of duty, adding features to the finished product that most people would never think of. This pursuit of excellence affects everything you do, from something as basic as writing a letter to something as complicated as closing a multimillion-dollar deal. You attend to every detail so that when it's finished, everyone who sees it says, "WOW! Now, *that's* amazing."

The pursuit of excellence isn't limited to work. If you're like most high-achieving women, you have your hands in everything that touches your life—and not just your hands, you throw your entire body and soul into it. You don't just volunteer for a cause you support, you lead the cause. You're not just a member of the PTA, you're president. Everything you touch seems to be made better by your involvement, and that's because everything you do, you do with the goal of making sure it's the best that it can be.

But sometimes this desire to excel goes a little too far along the continuum and ventures into the land of perfectionism. Not all high-achieving women are perfectionists, but many are or they are very close to it. Perfectionism is the extreme of striving for excellence. It takes the desire to excel and turns it into an inflexible expectation to excel.

Perfectionists are unnecessarily critical of themselves and they set unrealistically high expectations, not just for themselves but for others as well. They also have trouble walking away from something that is not exactly right. For example, they may stay up all night doing or redoing a project because it's not "perfect" or they may lie in bed, playing it over and over in their mind, thinking of ways to improve it. Although this may be fine for those rare individuals who don't have deadlines or don't need much sleep, it can be a source of endless pressure for high-achieving women whose schedules are bursting with commitments.

Failure is also an issue for perfectionists. To someone who strives for *excellence*, failure is disappointing. But to someone who expects *perfection*, failure is unacceptable and devastating. Perfectionists tend to overreact to every mistake, dwell on every flaw, and feel guilty and ashamed when they aren't able to produce a perfect product. And they don't just hold themselves to these impossible standards; they expect other people to be flawless as well, which, as you might imagine, can cause a great deal of conflict and tension in professional and personal relationships.

Although perfectionism is considered dysfunctional, and striving for excellence is not, both traits substantially increase stress levels. It may seem to others that you are capable of magic, but you're not magical. Those amazing feats you accomplish don't happen with a snap of your fingers. It takes real time and real energy to create excellence over and over, day in and day out. In fact, it takes a lot of real time and a lot of real energy, which, sooner or later, starts to run out. And that's what creates the *bad stress*—the self-induced pressure to excel in everything you do, every time you do it, in a world where time and energy aren't limitless.

There are other ways the pursuit of excellence (and, in the extreme, perfectionism) can impact stress levels. One is the tendency to do everything yourself because you know that if *you* do it, it will get done quickly and the end product will be excellent (or "perfect"). It's also likely that, in the past, you delegated a project to someone who either did it wrong or did it too slowly or didn't do it exactly as you would have done it. So you take back the project and decide to never "make that mistake again," which puts more work on your plate than necessary.

Another source of stress for those who strive for excellence is procrastination. By putting off a project until the last minute, you have less time to do the work, which means it probably won't turn out as well as it could have. When you finally turn in the work, there may be a slight sense of relief that it's off your plate, but the relief often doesn't outweigh the guilt or disappointment you feel from turning in work that is less than you're capable of. Over time, these feelings increase your stress level.

Finally, excellence isn't infinite. Even the tallest mountain has a peak. Once you're at the peak, there is nowhere else for you to go. Yet because you've created magic (excellence) so many times, there is an expectation that you can do it again and again and again. As clinical psychologist Steven Berglas writes in his book *Reclaiming the Fire*, "The notion that in an organization you are only as good as your last achievement is psychologically sound. A history of success heightens performance pressure by generating the expectation that a performer will meet or exceed past levels of achievement. In fact, merely to keep pace with the standards he has generated, a successful performer must either constantly improve or be judged wanting."[2] The question is: How can you improve on the best? The answer is *you can't*. However, "the best" is often expected (both by you and by others). And the result is *bad stress*.

Communication

High-achieving women are excellent communicators—except when it comes to their own needs. When most people experience crises in their lives, they reach out to friends, family, or sometimes even a professional for help. However, reaching out for help isn't something high-achieving women do very often. There are a few reasons why this is so.

First, if you're like most high-achieving women, crises are a normal part of your life, something you're used to handling. In fact, you probably don't even define the complicated and stressful situations you face as crises. If it's not a crisis in your mind, why would there be any need to talk about it, right? Just solve the problem and move on to the next one.

Except that over time, crisis after crisis can wear you down. Physiologically, the constant adrenaline rushes deplete your body. And psychologically, the mental strain associated with successfully negotiating and resolving every crisis can wear you down emotionally.

Another reason you may be reluctant to talk about stress is that you're cognizant of the fact that in just about everything you do, you are compared to men. If a man wouldn't ask for help, then why should you? If a man can stay at the office working until midnight, why shouldn't you? But just because a man does or doesn't do something, that doesn't mean it's right. Look at how often men drive around and around because they refuse to stop and ask for directions (yes, I know—I'm stereotyping). The reason many *people* don't ask is because they think asking questions might put them in a one-down position. But that's not a good reason, and neither is yours.

The reality is that when you keep your thoughts and feelings stuffed inside, you create a pressure cooker–type of atmosphere in your body. The pressure builds and builds inside with no place to go. And that results in *bad stress*.

Independence

Independence is a healthy state of being. However, many high-achieving women take independence to the extreme. If you're one of these women, you probably enjoy the freedom of working alone, and that's understandable. You can be creative. You can work at your super-speedy pace. You don't have to wait for anyone else to get something done. You don't have to worry about anyone else making a mistake. It's perfect, right? It might be if you had only one, two, three, or ten projects on the burner and a year to get them all done. But you likely don't have one, two, three, or ten projects. You may have a hundred projects, all going at the same time. But you can't let anyone else take some of the work because they won't do it as fast or as well as you would (see "striving for excellence"). So you don't delegate, which causes your to-do list to take up a notebook instead of a Post-it note. Plus, there's no reason you shouldn't be able to juggle a hundred sharp knives in the air at the same time. You're Superwoman, right? Wrong. So many high-achieving women have this

"Superwoman" script in their heads, telling them they should be independent enough or efficient enough or committed enough or (fill in the blank) enough to complete everything on their ever-growing to-do list. For some women I've worked with, their lists border on delusional (I wish I were joking).

Sally, a single mom of a tween and a teen and the vice president of business banking at a local bank, came to see me so I could help her be more efficient. The moment she sat down, she said, "I have a lot of things to do and I think that if I just learned to be more efficient, I could get them done more easily."

The session was prompted by Sally forgetting to attend an after-school meeting she had scheduled with her son and her son's teacher, which left her son "looking like an idiot" (as he described it) and Sally feeling guilty and embarrassed. "I just need to get my old efficiency back," she said. "I used to be the most efficient person around. I don't know what happened."

I started by asking Sally to take me through a typical day so I could understand her life a little better and figure out where we might be able to make some adjustments. It actually took close to the entire fifty-minute session for Sally to finish her list. She woke up at 5 a.m. to get the children's lunches made "because they like my lunches better than our housekeeper's." She jumped in the shower and dressed for work before the boys got up, which was around 6 a.m. The housekeeper came at 6 a.m., but Sally usually made the boys' breakfasts herself because they were "picky." She was the president of the Athletic Booster Club at her oldest son's school and the treasurer of the PTA at her youngest son's school. So on Tuesdays and Thursdays, she left the house right after breakfast to go to the schools to take care of any business she needed to attend to there.

Her job as a bank executive started at 9 a.m., but she tried to get in by 8:00 "to catch up." She usually left work by 6 p.m. to take her boys to their soccer practices or to catch at least one of their games, although she tried to make both if they were on the same night. As soon as the boys got home from soccer (which, between the two of them seemed to be just about every weeknight and on Saturdays), Sally made dinner while the boys pulled out their homework. In between the pasta and the sauce, she'd help them, while also returning e-mails, text messages, and phone calls that came in after hours. Once the boys showered and climbed into bed, Sally cleaned up from dinner, paid a few bills, caught up on the mail, tidied up around the house, and usually fell into bed around midnight.

In the few minutes left in that first session, I decided that some questions might shed a little more light on the problem. "How many meetings like this one have you missed?" I asked.

"That was the first one," she answered. "I never miss meetings. In fact, I'm always early."

"How many breakfasts have you missed making in the mornings?" I asked.

"I don't miss any," she said. "They need breakfast. It's not something that can be missed."

"And how many soccer games have you missed?"

"None, usually, unless, let's say one is playing at Independence Park and the other has a travel game in West Palm. But I get to most of them."

"Absent a lot from work? Miss many of your PTA or Athletic Booster Club meetings?"

"Never."

I sat silently for a few seconds.

"So what do you think?" Sally asked.

"I don't think I can help you with efficiency," I answered.

Sally sat there looking a little perplexed.

"But I thought that's what you did. Helped people become more efficient. Helped them organize their lives."

"I do, if that's what they need. But with everything you're juggling, you're about the most organized and efficient person I've ever seen. Do you think you might have come here for a different reason?"

I asked Sally not to answer right then, to think about my question and call if she wanted to meet again. A week later, she did and she began coming in regularly (on her lunch hour, not surprisingly, so she wouldn't miss anything else). As we explored the reasoning behind so many of the things she did, Sally discovered that much of it was related to the guilt she felt over the children not having a father in their lives. It made her feel like she needed to be both. So she spent time with the boys before and after school, but instead of it being quality time, it was rushed time.

Sally soon discovered that if she let the housekeeper do the job she hired her to do, like cooking and cleaning, she'd have more time to actually sit down with the boys, which accomplished two things: (1) By not racing around triple-tasking, she felt less stressed, and (2) She was able to enjoy quality time with the boys instead of being their chief, cook, and bottle washer (literally).

But that wasn't the only issue Sally needed to resolve. Her overly independent style resulted in many unnecessary things making their way onto her plate, and because she was an overachiever, she saw no reason why she shouldn't be able to do everything on it. In fact, this is such a common story among high-achieving women that some have started to call this type of behavior Superwoman Syndrome.[3]

But here's the problem. Sally wasn't Superwoman. And you're not either. Say it out loud if you have to. *I am not Superwoman.*

You see, Superwoman is a fictional character. If she weren't, she'd have been killed a few hundred episodes ago. No real person can save her world every day on a moment's notice. No real person can zip around her universe, accomplishing tasks at the speed of sound, crashing through obstacles in her path with her bare hands.

Real people actually have schedules and commitments. They can't just jump up when a crisis happens and fly off to fix it. They can't just blast through obstacles; they have to work around them. And they also have to sleep and eat and bathe and do all the other things humans do. Because of this, it's simply not possible to take on everything that makes its way into your life in a twenty-four-hour day, day after day, year after year, and not be killed by it—psychologically, and, yes, sometimes even physically.

So the moral of the story is that you can do a lot of things yourself, more than most can. And you can do most things better than everyone else. But that doesn't mean that you *should*. Being independent is one thing; being overly independent is another. We're back to that stress continuum, and it's the part of the continuum that leads to *bad stress*.

Commitment

High-achieving women commit. Then, they commit again. And then, they commit one more time. And then, another time. And each time they do, they inch a little farther along the commitment continuum until they get to the bright red, flashing lights surrounding overcommitment.

High-achieving women overcommit for so many different reasons and to so many different things that it's hard to keep up—for them as well as others. They overcommit to their jobs. They overcommit to causes. They agree to do favors for friends or colleagues. They volunteer to help at their child's school or a community organization (sometimes both). And while these acts—some selfless, some not—are certainly laudable, they can add hundreds of hours (and stress) to an already overscheduled life.

Overcommitment is often a consequence of poor limit setting, which is one of the biggest problems high-achieving women face. "Poor limit setting" means that you have trouble setting appropriate boundaries on your behavior or the behavior of others. In short, you have trouble saying *no*. A colleague calls for a favor, and you do it, even if you don't have the time. The boss asks you to accept a new assignment, and you accept it, even if you have no time in your schedule to devote to a new project.

For most women, the problem goes back to childhood. Most girls are socialized to be helpful, accommodating, and polite in groups. If they can help out, they are taught that they should, even if it pulls them away from something they're already doing or something they really wanted to do. And if they don't pull away to help, they're called selfish, uncaring, or self-centered, which usually leads to feelings of guilt over not being a "good girl."

When this happens, it teaches girls the roles they're expected to play in groups, and this can carry over into their relationships with adults. When someone needs help, that little girl in them is likely to say, "Sure," with a smile, even though it's pulling her away from something else she is doing.

But like most things in life, the tendency toward overcommitment can't be blamed entirely on childhood behaviors. Sometimes it's pride or the need for speed or the need for achievement that impels high-achieving women to take on too many responsibilities. Some women carry their spilling-out-of-the-sides planners like a badge of honor. Some men have their hot rods and sports cars; some women have their well-fed and well-nurtured planners.

Sometimes, conversely, it's insecurity that keeps high-achieving women from just saying no. What if I say no, and he thinks I can't keep up? Or what if I say no, and she gets mad at me? Or what if I say no, and they realize I'm in over my head? All are unhealthy fears. All lead to *bad stress*.

Perseverance

Like most of the other qualities discussed, perseverance is an excellent trait to have . . . except when it's time to give up. In every life, there are moments when, no matter how hard you try, no matter how much time you put into something, it just can't be done. But high achievers have a tough time admitting defeat. Again, there are a lot of reasons for this—not wanting to disappoint anyone, not wanting to show any sign of weakness—but when it's time to move on, it's time to move on. And to continue to work on something that can't be done is a waste of valuable time and causes *bad stress*.

Inflexibility

Flexibility—in the form of keeping an open mind or seeing things from a unique or new perspective—is usually associated with reduced stress. On the other hand, inflexibility—in the form of resisting change or being firm about what you like—is usually associated with increased stress. Unfortunately, high-achieving women tend to be a tad on the inflexible side. They grow accustomed to doing something the way they like to do it, and when someone does it differently, they either take it back and do it themselves or they get very tense and upset because it's not being done "right."

Maddy, a friend from college, used to be beyond inflexible when it came to her work as a researcher (fortunately she's made her way along the continuum to a better place now). She called me one day, fit to be tied, after one of her assistants set up an elaborate data collection form differently than the way Maddy had been setting it up for years.

"I showed her mine," she yelled into the phone. "I gave her all the data points. Got her into the spreadsheet. And an hour later, she came back with an entirely new form. I didn't even recognize it!"

"Was it correct?" I asked. There was a pause on the other end of the line. We psychologists tend to notice things like that.

"Technically," she finally answered, "I suppose it was correct if you mean could we have used it to collect the data. But it's not how I do it and I don't see why she felt she had to re-create the wheel. I should have just done it myself and then it would have been done right."

Of course, *right*, using Maddy's definition, means the way she did it. But the reality is that there is rarely only one right way to do something. So flipping out over something that's getting done, even if it's not getting done like you would do it, is counterproductive and leads to *bad stress*.

Responsiveness

For the same reasons as described in the overcommitment section, high-achieving women tend to be overly responsive to infringements on their time. This is best illustrated by Carmen, the business owner introduced in chapter 4. Carmen had this unwritten rule in her head that regardless of the day or hour, she had to respond to her e-mails and phone calls within an hour. Although clients and customers probably appreciate prompt responses, these kinds of unwritten rules are breeding grounds for *bad stress*.

Seriousness

High-achieving women tend to be very serious. And while there is nothing wrong with being serious when the situation calls for it, there's also something to be said for letting loose every once in a while and taking a lighter approach to work and life. Not everything is a crisis, not everything is a priority, not everything is Armageddon. To approach every day as if you're working at a nuclear power plant is not particularly healthy and it brings on a lot of *bad stress*.

So what's a high-achieving woman to do? You have a lot of amazing qualities, qualities that other people would love to have. It's just that sometimes these qualities are a little too far along their continuums, and this can create unnecessary stress. The key is to figure out which of the traits need adjusting and how to make those adjustments.

CHECKING YOUR GAUGES

We started out describing the unique qualities high-achieving women possess—qualities that sometimes cause them to travel a little too fast for the road conditions of their stress-filled lives. But if understood properly, these qualities can serve as gauges that you can check on a regular basis and adjust as necessary to help control your speed and reduce some of the stress in your life. By taking an *honest* look at each quality, you can narrow down the areas that are leading to the most stress and monitor these areas more closely.

Notice the emphasized word *honest*. It's hard for most people to honestly assess their strengths and weaknesses, but to read through this section with anything less than an honest appraisal of what needs to change will only lead to more trouble down the road. A good way to check your objectivity is to go through this section and write down the areas you think you need to work on. Then have someone who knows you really well—someone whom you trust—do the same thing: write down areas she or he thinks you need to work on. Then compare the two lists. If they're the same, you did a good job being honest with yourself. If there are some differences, talk through them and keep an open mind. Other people are often able to see your difficult areas before you are.

Striving for Excellence

Checking the Gauge: There's absolutely nothing wrong with striving for excellence, unless it's causing you too much stress. Putting pressure on yourself to get something done really well is what makes it turn out great; there's nothing wrong with that. So before you start tweaking, you first need to figure out if your pursuit of excellence is unhealthy. Here are a few questions that should help you answer that question:

- When you're working on a project, do you tell yourself that it has to be perfect before you present it or turn it in?
- Does it take you significantly more time to finish a project than it does your colleagues (assuming the project is similar in scope)?
- If there is a minor mistake or a slight flaw in a finished product, do you tear it down and start all over again?
- Do you overreact to mistakes or constructive criticism (can't sleep; obsessively think about it; are upset over a period of days as opposed to a period of minutes or hours)?
- Do you get upset when someone else's work isn't perfect?
- On ratings or scored projects, where you receive all high markings except one, do you ignore the higher markings and focus only on the lower marking?
- Does failure on a task cause you to think you are a failure?

If you answered *no* to most or all of these questions, you're probably not unnecessarily stressed by your pursuit of excellence and there's no need to make any adjustments. If, however, you answered *yes* to most or all of these questions, you probably need to consider making a few changes. Here are some suggestions that may help.

Reality Check Time: One of the first things you should consider is doing a reality check. A life without mistakes is impossible; there is no winnable, rational argument to the contrary. So to expect the impossible is setting yourself up for failure and only adds unnecessary stress to your life.

Learn from Your Mistakes: Not only is a mistake-free life impossible, it's impractical. How would we learn if we never made a mistake? Correcting mistakes and learning from them is how we move forward. So think back to times in the past when you've made a mistake. What happened? Were the consequences of the mistake catastrophic or was the problem easily resolved so that everyone moved on and soon forgot about it? Naturally, some mistakes are going to be bigger and more costly than others, but the majority of mistakes are easy to fix and are forgotten quickly. If everyone but you is able to move on, you need to ask yourself why.

Make Mistakes on Purpose: Another strategy you can try is to select a small, relatively insignificant project (don't start off with something big or important) and don't do your best on it. Just do a quick first draft and force yourself to not make any corrections. Then do a "worst-case scenario" assessment: make a list from worst to least of all the things that could happen by submitting the project in its current form. Then submit it. Often, nothing happens, and if something is said or done, it usually isn't even close to the worst-case scenarios at the top of your list. Doing this kind of exercise allows you to see firsthand that your fears about less-than-perfect work are unrealistic and are not worth the ongoing stress they cause.

Make a List: Another option is to review your work and make a list of what needs to be done to the best of your ability and what can be left at "good enough." If you're not sure, try to find out what your boss's expectations are. This way, you're not wasting valuable time perfecting work that only needs to be "good enough." You can then devote that extra time to other assignments or to improving the assignments that need to be exceptional.

Stop Procrastinating: If you're a procrastinator, you may want to consider asking your boss to give you deadlines that are earlier than the real deadlines (of course, the only way this will work is if your boss doesn't tell you what the actual deadline is). If you're your own boss, this can be quite a dilemma because it's hard to trick yourself into thinking a deadline is sooner than it really is; in this scenario, constant early reminders written into your calendar may help. If you have a partner, you may want to ask him or her to gently remind or constantly badger you (whichever works best for you) to begin working on the project.

Be Realistic in Your Expectations of Others: If one of your sources of stress is the imperfect work of others, make sure you're judging their work objectively and fairly. It's unfair to hold other workers who aren't high achievers to the standards you hold for yourself. Few people are going to be able to match your level of quality, speed, and thoroughness. To expect others to perform at your level, unless they're a peer at your same level, is to set them up for failure every time, which will create an unnecessary source of stress for both you and your coworkers. It also makes for strained relations with your coworkers, which can work against you in a professional setting and can create more stress.

It's also important to remember that everyone has a learning curve. Few people can pick up something and do it flawlessly the first time. So if you're someone who delegates and then immediately takes back the work the first time there is a mistake, you're not giving your staff or coworkers a fair opportunity to learn from their mistakes. It's unrealistic to give someone only one or even two chances to do something as accurately and as quickly as you would, when you've been doing it longer or have better knowledge of the work. The best solution is to continue to offer supervision for a reasonable period of time. One day is usually not reasonable, but "reasonable" should be based on the complexity of the task and the skill level of the worker doing it.

Find a New Peak: If you feel like you've reached the peak of your mountain and can't improve on what you're doing, maybe it's time to consider a transfer to a different division or to ask for a new challenge in your current job. It's difficult for high achievers to remain at status quo for too long. If the challenge is gone, it's hard to keep up your motivation and your energy for doing more of the same. If you're your own boss, look for new challenges inside or outside the business to keep from feeling stagnant. New challenges stimulate the brain and raise energy levels (but don't forget that you will likely have to give up on something old if you take on something new, unless you want your new peak to turn into a cliff that's so high you fall off the top!).

Seek Outside Assistance: If these suggestions don't offer any relief, you may want to consider bibliotherapy[4] (using books to help you discover ways to solve problems) or formal counseling. Sometimes perfectionism is a sign of Obsessive-Compulsive Personality Disorder, which requires more direct and individualized assistance than this book is able to provide.

Communication

Checking the Gauge: If you have open lines of communication with your colleagues and superiors; if you're comfortable approaching a colleague with a problem; if you don't feel isolated and alone at work; and if colleagues are willing to approach you and seek your advice, then communication is probably not a major source of stress for you. Here are a few questions to help you assess how communicative you are:

- When a crisis happens at work, do you prefer to handle it alone?
- If you have a question about something at work, do you prefer to check books, policy and procedure manuals, or other forms of written information to find the answer?
- Do you discourage or reject help when a colleague offers it?
- Do you tend to keep what happens at work away from your family?
- Do you worry that if you ask a question or ask for help that colleagues will see you as incompetent or inferior?

If you answered *yes* to these questions, you're probably keeping too much to yourself, which only adds to your stress. Consider making some of the adjustments described below to improve your connections.

Resist Jumping in and Fixing It: One reason why some high-achieving women feel isolated and alone is because they tend to handle everything on their own. When a problem arises and coworkers offer to help, the offer is rejected. A good way to overcome this is to resist the urge to jump in and fix a problem as soon as it happens. Instead, bring together a group of coworkers you think have the skills to handle whatever is happening and work together to come up with a solution. Open up a dialogue. You don't have to take their advice. In the end, you can still do what you would have done alone, but you might be surprised by what your colleagues can do and the ideas they can generate when you step aside and give them a chance to come up with solutions. It may be the case that they're too intimidated by you to step in and offer their suggestions without invitation because you always seem to handle everything so well on your own.

Share Outside of Work: Sharing is sharing, whether it's done in or out of the workplace. Talking to friends, family members, or colleagues about work-related problems has long been found to be an effective stress reducer, especially for women.

Independence

Checking the Gauge: Whether a high-achieving woman is too independent can be hard to gauge because different types of people handle workloads in different ways. But here are a few questions that may help you decide if you are too independent for your own good:

- Do you often feel overwhelmed with the amount of work you have?
- Do you regularly find it impossible to get all your work done?
- Do you rarely or never delegate?
- Do you quickly take back work you've delegated if it's not done to your satisfaction?
- Do you have a framed picture on your wall or desk saying, "If you want it done right, do it yourself"?
- Do you hold onto work that could be delegated because you can do it faster and better?
- Do you feel like you're Superwoman and can handle everything by yourself?

If you answered *yes* to most or all of these questions, you probably need to make some adjustments in your thinking in order to reduce your stress. The following suggestions might help.

Reality Check Time: Because you're so used to excelling—being the go-to person in your company, solving complex problems, getting things done faster and better than anyone else—you've probably convinced yourself that you're Superwoman and that you can perform this gig forever without help. But trust me: you really need to shred the Superwoman script. Why? Because it has a tragic ending. Any script that tells you that you should be available at a moment's notice, make no mistakes, quickly and effectively handle any problems that arise no matter how complex or sudden, and single-handedly juggle any number of sharp knives in the air without dropping any is going to end badly. At some point, if you don't share the load, those knives are going to come crashing down on your head.

Make Lists: Harriet Braiker, author of *The Type E* Woman*, recommends that women who are carrying too much on their plates make lists to help them redistribute the load. (In fact, many psychologists and time management experts recommend lists.) One of Braiker's suggestions is to make a list divided into three columns: Must Do Myself, Can Delegate with Supervision, and Can Delegate Completely. She then recommends that women use the list to delegate accordingly, without apology, making it clear to all those who receive work from the third column that the work is entirely their responsibility. Braiker also cautions that the supervision time for work from the second column should be as minimal as possible.[5]

I am a fan of lists. One of my favorites is a simple two-column list: What Must Get Done Today (ranked in order of priority) and What Can Wait. Lists are excellent ways to visualize your workload and to see at a glance what's critical, what's assignable to someone else, what's immediate, and what can be put off to another day. It's simply impossible to keep everything in your head, and if you try, you will inevitably forget something important. Another problem with keeping to-do lists in your head is that it's hard to keep the mental lists in any type of order. Nothing except the immediate task you're working on and possibly what needs to be done next is in any order. The result is that you often feel like there is an invisible burden hanging over your head, making you feel overwhelmed and scattered.

Lists also provide a good visual reinforcement of personal achievement. By crossing things off the list, you invoke a sense of accomplishment. Once a task is crossed off from the written list, it can be crossed off from your mind as well.

But for to-do lists to work, they have to be written in a way that doesn't cause them to become yet another source of stress. What do I mean? Well, if you're like a lot of people, the not-so-much-fun or the complex items on your to-do list keep getting pushed to the bottom until they can't be pushed down anymore because they're due tomorrow (or the next day or at some point that causes a time management crisis). Not such a good thing for reducing stress, is it?

To prevent this from happening, Gina Trapani, author of *Upgrade Your Life* and founding editor of Lifehacker.com, suggests that you have to know *how* to write to-do lists. She says that when you put off doing tasks on your list because they're complex, they're boring, or they make you feel overwhelmed at the thought of getting started, you need to check to see if you've confused *tasks* with *goals* and *projects*. Trapani writes, "A to-do is a single, specific action that will move a project toward completion. It's just one step. For example, 'Plan the committee lunch' is a project. 'E-mail Karen to get catering contract' is a to-do."[6] She suggests that by breaking down your to-do lists into smaller tasks, you will move closer to accomplishing the ultimate goal, and this will make the project seem much less overwhelming.

Trapani also suggests using action verbs and details when making your to-do lists. For example, instead of writing "Organize the going-away party," write the action you need to take with as many details as possible. For example, "Call Patty at ext. 3021 to send out e-mail invitations to all employees."

Do a Cost-Benefit Analysis: In the world of finance, one performs a cost-benefit analysis by analyzing a project or proposal to determine if the costs of doing the project are worth the benefits. In other words, you find, quantify, and add all the positive factors—the benefits—associated with the project, and then find, quantify, and subtract all the negative factors—the costs—of the project to see if it is worth doing.

You can perform a cost-benefit analysis with respect to your commitments and workload. Although you probably won't have actual numbers as you would in a financial scenario, you can still weigh the costs against the benefits in terms of stress, time, complexity, and interest on your part. Those responsibilities and commitments that are too "costly" should be delegated, reduced, or completely eliminated, if possible.

Focus: Another reason independent-minded workers feel so overwhelmed with work is that they allow too many interruptions during their workday. It's difficult to make a dent in your workload if you can't focus long enough to get projects handled and completed. So whatever you can do to negotiate blocks of time and focus on a single task, the more productive and the less stressed you're likely to be.

Terry, a writer, editor, and owner of a community-based magazine, puts a sign on her door when she doesn't want to be interrupted. The sign reads "I'm editing or writing. If the police are here, the office is on fire, or George Clooney calls or stops by, you can interrupt me. If not, please hold all questions until my door opens."

Terry said that she decided to put up the sign after she realized that her presence in the office was a stimulus for questions. "Whenever I was in the office," she said, "it seemed like there was one question after the next. I was constantly getting interrupted, and it was hard to get my work done. Then I noticed that on the days I was working on a story outside the office, my phone hardly ever rang, even if I was out the whole day. Apparently, whatever questions came up somehow got handled without me. It made me realize that just by being in the office I was a magnet for questions. So I put up the sign and it works like a charm."

Figure Out What You're Trying to Accomplish: With such a large number of responsibilities, it's important to honestly assess what you're trying to achieve. Then, look at what you're doing to achieve those things and see how effective your actions are in terms of accomplishing your goals. For example, let's say that one of your goals is to spend more time with your children, but you're like Sally, mentioned above, running around more than you're actually spending quality time with them. You need to adjust your actions to make them fit better with your ultimate goals. It's okay to want to be independent and assume responsibility for as much as you can, but if doing that adds more to your plate and burns you out, then it defeats the purpose.

Commitment

A few extra commitments, especially to important causes, such as schools or charities, can be a healthy addition to high-achieving women's lives, giving them a sense of pride and purpose beyond the workplace. However, over-commitment can take away all the positives and bring about many more negatives in the form of added burdens and stress.

Checking the Gauge:

- Do you feel like it's your job to help people in need—other than family members?
- Do you have difficulty saying *no*?
- Do you take on extra work even though you don't have time for it?
- Do you feel guilty when a colleague or friend asks for a favor and you can't help?
- Do you worry that you'll be judged negatively if you don't take on extra work?
- Do you worry that friends or colleagues will get mad at you if you tell them *no*?
- Do you feel a sense of pride when you're able to take on more commitments than anyone else, even though you know you don't have the time to complete everything?

If you answered *yes* to most or all of these questions, you probably have trouble setting appropriate limits with people in your life, and, as a result, you commit to more than you can reasonably handle. The following suggestions may be helpful.

Reality Check Time: Helping everyone may give you a great sense of accomplishment and pride, but will your friends, colleagues, and family members really think less of you if you don't sell a record number of pizza discount cards for the school fundraiser—or will they simply be appreciative of your effort? Will your children be upset or disappointed in you if you aren't president of the PTA—or will they just be happy that you joined and attend meetings every now and then? The reality is that you probably already do so much that no one would think less of you if you stepped back a bit from a particular project or cause. Often, your expectations of yourself are higher than anything anyone else would ever come close to expecting.

A friend of mine, Susan, saw this happen firsthand with a fellow volunteer at her daughter's school. "Her son was new to the school," Susan said, "and she came on full force. If we were having a bake sale, she not only volunteered to bring brownies, she also volunteered to bring cupcakes, make the posters, bring tablecloths, and bring cash for change. If we sponsored a fair, she took on the lion's share of the work to organize it."

Everyone in the PTA loved her involvement and commitment to the school, but they also noticed that the woman never seemed to be enjoying herself. "She was always rushing around," Susan said, "making phone calls to take care of last-minute details that I honestly don't think anyone would have even noticed if they weren't there. It was burnout in the making." So Susan pulled together a few of the other volunteers, and they decided to do an "intervention." They sat her down one day when she was looking particularly frazzled and told her that they really appreciated what she was doing and that she was an enormous asset to the school's volunteer program, but they were worried that she was taking on too much and didn't seem to be enjoying any of it. They told her that they were just happy having another set of helping hands. No one expected her to do everything.

Susan said she could almost see the weight lift off the woman's shoulders. After that, she still did more than most, but she didn't take on every project as if it were a life-or-death situation. And she actually started enjoying herself. Susan's story is a great example of how your expectations of yourself may be completely out of proportion to what other people are expecting when you take on a project. Sometimes it's more important to simply enjoy whatever you can do rather than stressing out over making it perfect.

Practice Saying No: Sometimes you may commit to something because you're caught off guard when the favor is asked and, off the top of your head, you don't have a good reason to say no. Actually, you don't need a good reason to say no. But if you feel like you do, then it helps to be prepared, and the only way to be prepared is to practice. Think of situations that have come up in the past and then experiment with polite ways to say "No, thank you." For example, you can practice with "That sounds like a really good cause, but I don't have the time to devote to it," "Thanks for thinking of me, but I can't. Sorry," or "I'm sorry. I don't have any room in my schedule for another commitment." If it makes you feel better and you can do it right at that moment, you might even recommend someone else to do the job. For example, you might say, "I don't really have time to take on another client, but my associate is accepting new cases."

Negotiate: If you really feel strongly about the project or cause but don't have the time right then to devote to it, you always can negotiate a time that will work better for your schedule. For instance, while I was writing this book, a client called to see if I was available to consult on a new case. The case sounded interesting, and I had worked with the client before and liked her, but I knew I wouldn't have the time to devote to the case until after my submission deadline. So I negotiated for more time by saying, "I don't have any time in my schedule right now to take on any new cases, but if you can wait until April, I could take the case then."

If you do this, though, make sure that when you're negotiating you don't cut the deadline too close. If anything, negotiate for more time than you'll need; that way, if you're available earlier, the client (or whoever) will be happy and you'll feel less stressed. Most important, be prepared to walk away with a "No, thank you" if the time can't be worked out. For example, if the client who had contacted me hadn't been able to wait until April, I wouldn't have caved in and taken the work. I would have simply referred her to another psychologist.

Perseverance

It's great to hang in there, except when there is no realistic chance of winning.

Checking the Gauge:

- Do you believe that you should never give up?
- Do you have trouble admitting defeat?
- Do you believe that there is always a solution to a problem?
- Do you believe that giving up is a sign of weakness?

If you answered *yes* to all or most of these questions, your diligence in some areas of your life may be causing you to struggle and stress for no good reason. Here are some suggestions that may help you move past the problem.

Reality Check Time: There are some situations that are so complicated or problematic they can never be resolved. There are some problems for which there are no solutions, and even if there were a solution, there are some circumstances in which finding it wouldn't be worth the time. In these situations, you just need to give up and move on.

Get a Second Opinion: If you're extremely diligent and have trouble giving something up, it's a good idea to get a second opinion as to whether it's worth the time and trouble to keep struggling to find a solution. Maybe that person will see the problem from a new perspective and find the solution for you. Maybe that person will come up with an idea you didn't consider that will lead you to the answer. But if the second opinion confirms that there is no solution or that it's just not worth the time, the best course of action is to let it go and spend your valuable time working on something else.

Inflexibility

Cognitive flexibility is one of the best weapons to have in your arsenal when it comes to fighting back against stress in your life. By being more open to new or different ideas, you're more likely to discover ways to solve problems you've never considered before. Flexibility can also help you adjust more easily to changes in your environment, which is one of the biggest stressors in people's lives. To see where you stand on the flexibility continuum, ask yourself the following questions:

Checking the Gauge:

- Do you tend to resist change?
- Do you have trouble admitting that you're wrong?
- Do you want everyone to do things the way you do them?
- Do you think there is only one right way to do most things?
- Do new procedures at work cause you to feel upset or anxious?

If you answered *yes* to most or all of these questions, inflexibility may be stretching you too thin. Here are some ideas to help you change that.

Retrain Your Brain: Many wildly successful products and ideas were created by people who kept an open mind and looked at things from a new or unique perspective. Just because something works the way you're doing it doesn't mean there aren't other ways it would work just as well. Train your brain to see beyond what works and what doesn't work for you. Don't immediately dismiss new ideas or fresh ways of approaching old problems without giving them a chance. Part of this approach will require that you redefine "right" to mean "if it works" instead of "what works for me." What's the harm? You can always use what works for you without dismissing the possibility that a different way might work better for someone else or even for you, eventually.

Responsiveness

Every company loves responsive employees, but it's important to keep in mind the old saying "Too much of a good thing can be harmful to your health." Being available 24/7 has its costs.

Checking the Gauge:

- Are you overly responsive to demands made upon your time?
- Do you feel like your time is less important than your boss's, your clients', or your colleagues' time?
- Are you "connected" all the time?

If you answered *yes* to most or all of these questions, your constant availability may be killing you. Here are some ideas to consider to keep from blowing out, burning out, becoming ill, or worse—dying.

Set Limits: If you feel like you have little control over your time and your life because you're always worried about being available to others, the only way to fix this is to set appropriate limits, not just on others but on the devices that make you so accessible. For suggestions on how to take back control of your life, see the solutions offered at the end of chapter 4.

Seriousness

Actor Alan Alda once said, "When people are laughing, they're generally not killing each other."[7] Good point.

Checking the Gauge:

- Do you rarely laugh?
- Do you believe that work is a place where you should always be serious?
- Do you think it's inappropriate to have fun at work?

If you answered *yes* to most or all of these questions, you may be taking yourself too seriously. Lighten up a little. The following suggestions can get you started.

Reality Check Time: Even in the most stress-filled, dangerous, and serious workplaces in the world, there are light moments. It's human nature to laugh and have some fun, relaxing moments, and that includes, when appropriate, moments at work.

Laugh: Just laugh. It doesn't get any more basic than that. Laughter is a great stress reliever. It's good for you physically and mentally. It's contagious. It's even good to laugh at yourself every once in a while.

Ask What Purpose It Serves: Most high-achieving women are practical. If they do something, it's because it serves a purpose. So ask yourself: What purpose does being serious serve? Will it help me do my job better? Does my boss need to see me as serious all the time? The answer is almost always *no*. In fact, being too serious can actually interfere with your work because constant seriousness can lead to increased depression, anxiety, and stress. There are times when you need to be serious, but that's not all the time.

PREPARE FOR RESISTANCE

Whichever of these adjustments you make, the end result will likely be positive change that reduces your stress. But be prepared for resistance. Making changes in the way you think and the way you act is likely to be difficult not only for you but also for the people in your life. Just as you've been reinforced in many different ways to follow your high-achieving style, other people in your life have been reinforced by your behavior as well, sometimes over a period of years. Once you do your cost-benefit analyses and figure out what you're going to change, whatever "that" is, is very likely going to affect someone else. In other words, when you stop doing certain things, someone else is going to have to pick up the slack. But if we're anything as humans, we're resilient. If you stay focused and do what you need to do, in time, the people in your life will do what they need to do.

KEEP YOUR EXPECTATIONS REALISTIC

Many of the stressors in your life are so deeply embedded into your mind and into your patterns of behavior that it's unrealistic to expect that change will come overnight. But like anything else, practice makes perfect. Now that you have a better understanding of what your challenges are, you're in a better position to face them head-on and make the necessary adjustments to reduce your stress level. But be patient and give yourself a realistic amount of time to adapt to the changes you're making (two things that are often difficult for high-achieving women to do).

We all fall into habits, and as those habits get reinforced, they grow stronger. But this can work to your benefit. As you make changes that will free up more of your time and reduce your stress, that extra time and the reduction in stress will become a reinforcement of its own. There will always be slip-ups and reversions to old ways of thinking and doing, but with focus and persistence, like everything else in your life, you can do this and do it well.

PART TWO:

GET SET

Chapter 6

ENGINE CHECK:
Gauging Your Stress Level

Engine Check: *a diagnostic check to determine if any*
component or system of the engine is not working properly.
—from RepairPal.com

At this point, we've surveyed the scene, figured out what kinds of things throw you off-course, and pinpointed some ways to anticipate and avoid these obstacles in the future. The next step is to check your engine and see what, if any, damage you've suffered at this stage of your race.

Up to this point, we've explored, in a general way, the various types of stress that commonly affect high-achieving women. Now it's time to assess where you are on the burnout continuum. Some of you are at the starting line, and you're reading this book to be in a better position to anticipate and prevent problems in the future. Others of you will be farther along, experiencing varying degrees of stress but still managing fairly well. And still others will be burned out and will have either left the race or are desperate to find a way to leave.

For those of you who are just starting out, use this section to familiarize yourself with the warning signs of stress and burnout so that when symptoms first start appearing, you'll recognize them and act quickly to put some buffers in place to relieve them. For the rest of you, this section will help you figure out where you are along the stress/burnout continuum. It also should help you figure out how much engine damage you've suffered and what kind of repairs you'll need to make so that you can get back up to speed. The first step is to understand exactly what stress does to your body.

THE IMPACT OF STRESS ON THE BODY

Stress is a normal physiological reaction to a perceived physical or psychological threat. When we sense a threat, our bodies react in a way that helps us defend against it, using an instinctual self-protective mechanism. This reaction, labeled the "fight-or-flight" response by physiologist Walter Cannon in the early twentieth century, is involuntary. Our bodies do it automatically and immediately whenever we sense danger in our environment. It sets into motion a complex series of physiological events designed to help us survive the threat.[1]

Internally, the sympathetic nervous system responds by releasing a flood of adrenaline, which prepares our bodies to react quickly to fend off or escape the danger. Endorphins are released to temporarily increase our threshold for pain. Blood vessels in our skin constrict to prevent potential blood loss. Sweat glands open to cool our hardworking bodies. Blood flow is diverted from less vital systems, like the digestive system and the kidneys, to more vital organs like the heart. Heart rate increases, muscles tighten, and blood pressure rises. Breathing becomes more rapid, helping to bring more oxygen to our muscles. Our senses become sharper, and our focus increases. This in turn improves our reaction time and increases our strength and stamina.

All these things occur within seconds to significantly increase our chances of surviving a life-threatening event or of helping someone else survive a life-threatening event. Once the threat is gone, our system returns to homeostasis. Or at least that's the way it's supposed to work.

From an evolutionary perspective, this fight-or-flight response was very adaptive in the sense that it kept our ancient ancestors from being attacked and killed by wild animals. In more modern times, not so much. The response is still helpful in those situations in which we need to escape a dangerous situation (like maneuvering safely through a busy intersection on foot) or to focus on an important task (like a big exam). But very little of the stress we experience today is due to a mortal threat.

The problem is, our bodies can't tell the difference. From a physiological perspective, a threat is a threat, mortal or otherwise. So whether we're trapped in a ravine with a hungry mountain lion or trapped in our office with a ferociously overflowing in-box, the body's response is the same—prepare for battle.

That would probably be okay if we could run out of our offices (the "flight" response) to escape the ferocious in-box or smash it to bits with a club (the "fight" response). But we can't. We just have to suck it up and adjust. We also can't throw our computer out the window when the Internet is running slowly, although that would probably make us feel good. We just have to sit there and wait and wait and wait and . . . you get the picture. The body just keeps reacting to all these "threats," and there's no real chance for it to return to normal. Simply put, the body isn't designed to handle that much stress for that long a period of time.

Endocrinologist Hans Selye, recognizing that prolonged stress produces a pattern of reactions in the body that can lead to increased infections, illnesses, and sometimes even death, developed a model he called the General Adaptation Syndrome (GAS) to describe and explain this process. The GAS has three stages. The first stage, the Alarm Reaction, is basically the fight-or-flight reaction described by Cannon. The second stage, called Resistance, is the phase in which the body tries to adapt to the stress to prevent illnesses and infections. This causes our immune system to kick into overdrive. But it can't do this indefinitely, which leads to the third stage, Exhaustion. Exhaustion results when the body's resources become depleted by too much stress.[2] On a physiological level, the body basically burns out, which is why exposure to chronic stress can lead to serious health and emotional problems or can exacerbate preexisting conditions.

WHAT HAPPENED TO "TEND AND BEFRIEND"?

Being the detail-oriented women that you are, you're probably scratching your head and thinking, "Wait a minute. Didn't she say earlier that this whole fight-or-flight reaction is a man thing?"

Yes, I did. And it is. Sort of.

Earlier I described a study out of UCLA that discovered that fight-or-flight isn't the typical way women respond to stress. The study found that when faced with a threat, women are predisposed toward a "tend and befriend" response.[3] Basically, our instinct is to take care of our children, circle the wagons with female friends, and build connections with other women. This was found to be a much healthier way to cope with stress—we would probably all agree with this. Except, how often do high-achieving women actually find themselves in these types of situations?

Think about it. If you have children, they usually aren't with you at work, and even if they were, the "threats" that you experience on the job aren't to your children, so there is no need to protect them. In the days of the woolly mammoths, this probably made sense. The physically stronger males would go out and fight off the threat or they would flee while the women circled the children and found a safe place to hide. But that's not the world we live in today.

The high-achieving women I know don't have many opportunities to affiliate with friends and build and nurture networks with other women in the workplace. First, the excessive work and life demands of high-achieving women don't leave a lot of time for affiliating, building, and nurturing much of anything. And second, in the workplaces where high-achieving women tend to gravitate, there aren't ample opportunities to connect with other women even if they wanted to. The reality is that for those women who have climbed highest on the ladder of success, they often find themselves alone in what is very much a man's world.

In *Why Women Should Rule the World*, Dee Dee Myers tells a story about an experience Katie Couric had shortly after she was hired to anchor the *CBS Evening News*. Couric was invited to the White House for a briefing on a speech the president was going to give later that evening. Although Couric was struck by the "awe-inspiring" surroundings of the White House, she apparently was equally as struck by the fact that, aside from some women working as support staff, she was, as Myers describes it, "the only person in the room—from either the press or the administration—wearing a skirt." Myers adds, "I'd been in her pumps, so to speak. While I was White House press secretary, I participated in a number of similar briefings before major presidential events. I was often the only woman in the room."[4]

I know of no research today that shows how women react when their predisposed responses aren't available to them, but from what I've seen, it would seem that the Alarm/Resistance/Exhaustion model discovered by Hans Selye is what these high-achieving women are experiencing. So once again, women are hit with a double whammy. The healthy response that women are predisposed to have when we're faced with stress isn't typically available to us in the environments we work in, and the default response is slowly killing us.

INDIVIDUAL DIFFERENCES

We don't all respond to stress in the same way. We each have our own trigger points for stress. People who are more laid-back tend to have higher trigger points before the fight-or-flight response kicks in, whereas those who are more edgy or sensitive tend to have lower trigger points.

Our specific reactions to stress are also different. Some people experience headaches and depression; others develop ulcers and anxiety. Some use stimulants to stay awake and alcohol to fall asleep. Others yell, worry, or cry. But in general, reactions to stress can be broken down into physical symptoms, psychological difficulties, and negative behavioral changes.

Stress can also be mediated by a number of different factors unique to our individual circumstances. For example, people who have strong social support networks—friends, family, and colleagues they can count on to help them through tough times—tend to be more resistant to the effects of stress. Personality also plays a role. And interestingly, knowledge about stress can mediate its impact. Simply being educated about the nature of stress, its impact, and ways to reduce it increases the likelihood that we will act in ways to decrease our stress (which is why it's good that you're reading this book).

WARNING LIGHTS

When I talk with burnout victims and we go back over their lives to see what got them to that point, we inevitably discover that there were warning lights. Some that they missed; some that they saw and decided not to attend to. But they were always there, usually flashing brightly but often ignored.

Physical Signals of Stress

Just as a car sends out warning signals to the driver when it's moving too fast, our bodies often provide the first cues to us that our stress levels are too high. This is because, from a physiological perspective, our bodies are the first to experience the stress. When stress throws us off-balance physically, our bodies react with signals to let us know that something is wrong.

The problem is that most of us ignore these signals and continue to go about our busy lives. In fact, we're quick to find reasons to prove that the signals we're receiving from our bodies aren't serious. We say things like, "Oh, I just didn't sleep well last night, that's all. I'll be fine tomorrow" or "It's probably just something I ate. I'm okay."

So let's look at the most commonly reported physical symptoms associated with stress in the hope that if and when they appear in your life, you'll recognize them and take quick action.

Fatigue: One of the first physical signs of stress is fatigue, which shouldn't be surprising, given all the stressors we've noted—work demands, long hours, household and family responsibilities, and the other miscellaneous commitments that high-achieving women take on. In fact, according to a recent survey conducted by the American Psychological Association (APA), 35 percent of women report experiencing fatigue several times a week (compared to 25 percent of men).[5] But because fatigue is so common these days, and because it's not thought of as "serious," it's often ignored as a symptom of stress, not just by women but by medical professionals as well.

Sleep Problems: Closely related to fatigue are sleep problems. According to a recent study conducted by the National Sleep Foundation, 67 percent of women experience sleep problems at least a few nights a week, and 43 percent say that daytime sleepiness interferes in their daily activities. Yet few of these women are going to bed earlier. Over two-thirds of the women studied associated their sleep problems with stress, yet when pressed for time, over half reported that sleep is the first thing they give up. Instead, 60 percent catch up on household chores, 37 percent spend time with their children, 36 percent spend time on the Internet, and over 20 percent perform job-related activities at least a few nights a week.[6]

This is not only unfortunate, it's dangerous for women's health. Of those who reported experiencing sleep problems nightly or almost nightly, 31 percent are classified as obese, 38 percent reported driving drowsy at least once a month, and 43 percent said that they use sleep aids at least a few nights a week.[7] Sleep deprivation has also been linked to decreased reaction time, decreased speed and accuracy, slower processing speed, impaired decision making, depression, anxiety, and a weakened immune system, among other things.

Chest Pain or Heart Palpitations: Chest pain is obviously not unique to stress. In fact, there are many reasons someone may experience chest pain, including indigestion, heartburn, referred pain from the spine, pneumonia, bronchitis, and, of course, the most serious, heart attack. Because of the potential for serious consequences, chest pain requires immediate medical attention. If, after a thorough medical assessment, there is no evidence of heart disease or any other physical condition as the cause, the most likely culprit is stress. In fact, when you understand the body's physiological response (the fight-or-flight response) to stress, the symptom of chest pain is understandable. Physically, our bodies respond with a flood of adrenaline into our bloodstream, the tightening of the chest muscles, increased respiration, and increased blood flow to the heart (which, in some cases, can actually cause a heart attack in someone who doesn't even have heart disease).

Headaches: Headaches are one of the most common symptoms of stress, especially in women. According to the APA poll previously referenced, women are much more likely to report headaches linked to stress than are men (56 percent versus 36 percent).[8] Tension headaches are commonly linked to stress, and some research suggests that migraines may be, as well. A survey conducted by the American Headache Society found that the triggers most commonly cited by migraine sufferers were physical and emotional stress.[9]

Lightheadedness: A quick rise or drop in heart rate or blood pressure can result in a feeling of lightheadedness. Like chest pain, lightheadedness should be medically evaluated, as it may be a sign of an underlying medical condition, such as heart disease or low blood pressure. But since heart rate and blood pressure are directly affected by stress, dizziness and lightheadedness are commonly reported by those who experience chronic stress.

Gastrointestinal Discomfort: In part, because our physiological reaction to stress results in resources being diverted from the digestive system, prolonged stress can lead to a variety of gastrointestinal problems. Commonly reported symptoms include indigestion, stomachaches, stomach cramps, nausea, constipation, and diarrhea. In fact, 18 percent of women in the APA study reported upset stomach or indigestion associated with stress.[10] And although medical conditions such as irritable bowel syndrome and ulcerative colitis are not believed to be caused by stress, stress is believed to exacerbate these conditions.[11]

Gynecological Problems: Numerous studies have found a link between stress and female infertility. Sarah Berga, a reproductive endocrinologist at Emory University, has discovered that high levels of stress hormone prevent ovulation and therefore conception. Her most recent study, funded by the National Institutes of Health (NIH), found that those most at risk are women who demand too much of themselves.[12] Dr. Berga says, "It's not really their jobs, it is the way they approach life—we don't want to discourage women's ambitions as much as help them develop realistic expectations. Our studies have found that women perform better in their demanding jobs and other roles when they have better attitudes about not being perfect."[13]

Although few of the women in Dr. Berga's study reported experiencing stress, she believes this is because many high-achieving women are not aware of how stressed they really are. She explains, "Just asking women if they are stressed doesn't always lead to an accurate answer, in part because some people are not aware of how stressed they are. Often it is those around them who know best." She believes that women often have unrealistic attitudes about themselves and others, and that they "think they can get more done in the day than is realistic, which causes them to feel as if they are underperforming even when they are not."[14]

Menstrual irregularities, such as amenorrhea and endometriosis, have also been linked to stress. These medical conditions can result in an enormous amount of stress in women's lives. Excessive menstrual bleeding and the pain that often accompanies it can make it difficult for women to do things that are normally taken for granted, such as going to the store. Work is also interrupted by these kinds of problems, not just because of the symptoms themselves but also because of the distractions they cause. Sometimes the bleeding is so heavy that women can't even leave the house, and when no medical explanation can be found, women are often left feeling helpless, hopeless, and extremely frustrated.

Behavioral Signals of Stress

Stress not only negatively impacts our bodies, it also can dramatically affect how we interact with our environment and how we react to various situations, including situations that may seem inconsequential to most people. For example, someone under a lot of stress may completely flip out over a minor error in a report or being served a baked potato at lunch instead of french fries.

One of the first indicators *to other people* that someone is stressed is the behavioral changes they see. While a husband may not notice his wife's heart palpitations, lightheadedness, or indigestion, he almost certainly will notice changes in the way she's acting. In fact, other people may well see these changes before the person experiencing the stress sees them.

Many high-achieving women become defensive when a family member or friend mentions these kinds of changes. But it's important to listen to their comments with an open mind. They may not always be right about what they're "seeing," but you may not always be right either.

So let's take a look at the most common behavioral changes associated with stress.

Change in Eating Patterns: Stress can impact eating patterns in two ways, both of which can have significant psychological and physical consequences for women. In fact, one of the most common ways women respond to stress is through overeating, also called comfort eating. This can lead to dangerous health problems, including weight gain and obesity, as well as feelings of embarrassment, guilt, and shame, which are commonly reported by overweight women.

Recently, researchers at Pennsylvania State University with the support of NIH discovered that stress hormones may actually play a significant role in overeating. Their study found that cortisol, one of the hormones released when we're stressed, acts as a mediator between obesity and depression in girls—but, interestingly, not in boys. An article describing the study says, "Although it is not clear why high cortisol reactions translate into obesity only for girls, scientists believe it may be due to physiological and behavioral differences—estrogen release and stress eating in girls—in the way the two genders cope with anxiety."[15]

But stress can cause the opposite to occur as well. Many women report a loss of appetite during periods of stress. They just don't feel like eating, which in the short-term deprives cells of the calories they need to supply energy to their bodies, and in the long-term weakens their immune system.

Eating disorders, such as anorexia and bulimia, are also believed to have strong links to stress. Dr. Jacalyn Robert-McComb, a professor of exercise physiology at Texas Tech University and an expert on the physiological aspects of stress, reports that research has consistently found that females with eating disorders report higher levels of stress in their lives than those without eating disorders. She indicates that one aspect of stress in the lives of women today is the comparisons they make between how they look and how society expects women to look, in large part because of the media.

Dr. Robert-McComb says, "Stereotypes of what women should look like are pervasive in the media and most women do not fit the stereotype. Even those who do fit the stereotype sometimes do not perceive themselves as fitting the stereotype."[16] This scenario creates negative thoughts and increased stress in their lives. When stressors such as these and others get to the point where women's lives begin to seem out of control, some turn to food. Being able to decide how much or how little they eat is one way to feel a sense of control, which can mark the beginning of an eating disorder.

Increase in Drug or Alcohol Use: In an attempt to deal with stress and the symptoms commonly associated with it, such as insomnia and depression, many high-achieving women are turning to alcohol and drugs, including caffeine, tobacco, and prescription medication. Many women report needing excessive amounts of caffeine just to make it through their day, and some turn to "uppers" to get through. On the other end of the spectrum, "downers" such as alcohol or sleeping pills, are often used to help overstressed women fall asleep or temporarily escape the harsh realities of their lives.

In fact, prescription medication abuse has become increasingly popular among high-achieving women. In a recent MSNBC article, contributor Karen Asp, citing data from the National Institute on Drug Abuse, reports that close to 6 percent of adult American women (about 7.5 million) say they use prescription medications "for a boost of energy, a dose of calm or other nonmedical reasons." Asp says this dangerous trend may be the result of what I've previously referred to as Superwoman Syndrome. "Overworked, overwhelmed and overscheduled women," she writes, "juggling families, friends, and careers are turning to stimulants, painkillers, and antianxiety meds to help launch them through endless to-do lists."[17]

This, of course, can end very badly. An arrest for drug possession or prescription fraud can have severe and sometimes irreparable repercussions. Job loss, revocation of professional licenses, divorce, and loss of custody of one's children are all serious consequences I have witnessed firsthand in the lives of high-achieving women with substance abuse problems.

Even when drug use is legal, it can still lead to both physical and psychological dependence. Because they have a prescription, many women don't consider the overuse of medication as abuse, yet they are likely to hide the problem from family and friends. In fact, it's often not until a critical incident occurs, such as an arrest, an overdose, or the worst-case scenario of death, that the extent of the problem is revealed.

Hyperemotionality: One of the most obvious signs of stress is a dramatic change in mood. These mood changes can come in many different forms. Uncharacteristic outbursts, impatience, and a shortened temper can often lead to tension in personal and professional relationships. Equally troublesome are periods of excessive crying, fidgeting, or nervousness. Symptoms such as these tend to feed the stereotype that women are psychologically unstable and unable to handle the strain of a demanding career. Unfortunately, there is little to no recognition that the stress of working in a hostile, gender-biased workplace is what drives women to these hyperemotional states in the first place.

Poor Concentration/Attention and Forgetfulness: Memory problems and difficulty focusing and concentrating are commonly reported symptoms of stress. Jumping from one task to another, not finishing projects, and having to repeatedly ask for directions or explanations are all behavioral manifestations of stress. These symptoms are often caused by fatigue and loss of sleep, which can become a vicious cycle. As a woman's performance and productivity suffer, her stress increases.

Loss of Interest: Loss of interest in activities or people that were once important is a common symptom of depression, but it can also be brought on by stress. Behavioral manifestations may include not wanting to go to work, not wanting to spend time with family or friends, loss of interest in sex, or not wanting to take part in activities that once were enjoyable, such as sports, going to movies, or going on vacations. Other signs of loss of interest often seen in the workplace are procrastination, increased absenteeism, chronic tardiness, and not returning e-mails or phone calls.

Isolation: Isolation is often a consequence of losing interest in people and in life in general. It can take the form of wanting to be alone, closing doors to keep people out, being generally inaccessible, always eating alone, not returning e-mails or phone calls, or being a poor team player.

Increase in Nervous Habits: Stress is often reflected by an increase in nervous habits. Nail biting, teeth grinding, fidgeting, hair pulling, foot tapping, leg shaking, hair twisting, and lip biting are all common examples of nervous habits sometimes brought on by stress.

Psychological Signals of Stress

Just about any psychological symptom known to the field of psychology can be a sign a stress; however, there are a few symptoms that are most commonly linked to it.

Depression: Depression is one of the most commonly diagnosed problems in America. It affects millions of people each year and is particularly problematic for women. According to an APA report, *Summit on Women and Depression*, women are more than twice as likely as men to suffer from a major depressive episode in their lifetime.[18] Although many factors can cause depression, life stress is certainly one of the most common. According to the APA report, more than 80 percent of community cases of major depression were preceded by a stressful life event.[19]

Depression is often thought of as the normal sadness or loneliness we all experience at some point in our lives, and that certainly is one kind of depression. However, clinical depression is much more severe and debilitating than just the normal and appropriate sadness everyone experiences. Symptoms can include fatigue and loss of energy; feelings of guilt, worthlessness, helplessness, hopelessness, and/or pessimism; sleep problems; irritability; restlessness; loss of interest in activities or hobbies once pleasurable; overeating or loss of appetite; and/or thoughts of suicide or suicide attempts.

Anxiety and Worry: Anxiety and worry are classic signs of stress. In fact, in the previously cited APA stress study, 55 percent of women (compared to 43 percent of men) reported symptoms of anxiety and nervousness.[20] Anxiety, like depression, can be fleeting and situational or it can be chronic and debilitating. Symptoms of clinical generalized anxiety can include restlessness, fatigue, sleep problems, concentration and attention problems, irritability, and physical symptoms (such as headaches, muscle tension, or shortness of breath).

Feelings of Hopelessness and Helplessness: When we experience stressful events continually and with little respite, it is not unusual to feel helpless and hopeless. In high-achieving women, these feelings are often brought on by a sense that, regardless of what they do or how hard they try, the stress does not let up. These feelings, coupled with the sense of loss of control, are commonly cited precursors to burnout.

HOW MUCH IS TOO MUCH?

Because of the serious consequences, it's important to be aware of the common signs and symptoms of stress and to try to figure out where you stand—to give yourself an engine check, so to speak. However, it's not always easy to determine how much stress is "too much." Because people have different personalities, life experiences, thresholds, and mediators for stress, there is no magic number of signals that will tell you if your stress level has exceeded your body's capacity to handle it.

Of course, common sense says that the more symptoms you have, the worse your stress is and the more dangerous it is to your physical and psychological health. And I agree with that to some extent. But let me offer a word of caution about relying too heavily on numbers: they can be misleading. Who is to say that a woman who suffers from debilitating headaches due to the incessant, unyielding stress in her life is any less stressed or at risk for burnout than someone who experiences ten of the symptoms in a milder form?

The point is that it's not for me or anyone else to judge the extent to which stress is impacting your life. You're smart. You're well informed (if you weren't before, you are now). And you know when something is interfering with your ability to be productive, to enjoy life, to feel the passion you once did. In the past (and maybe still), you might have denied these symptoms, blown them off as something that would pass in time. But now you know the whole story.

You know what's happening to your body as a result of stress and you know what's happening to your mind. And if you feel that the stress you're experiencing is too much, whether you have one of these symptoms or all of them, you need to do something about it—now. Because if you don't, it's only a matter of time before you're going to experience that "everything I never wanted" moment. Like Athena, your engine is going to burn out.

Chapter 7

RUNNING ON EMPTY:
Gauging Where You Are on the Burnout Continuum

Running on Empty: *This idiom refers to a car running when the gas gauge indicates it is out of fuel.*
—from Dictionary.com

S o let's recap. You gravitate toward jobs that were created by men and for men where you regularly confront gender-biased obstacles that put you at a disadvantage. Your hours are exceptionally long, your work-load is exceedingly heavy, and the performance pressures you face are enormously high. The technology you use to get your job done makes your workday practically endless. Society punishes you for your ambition, your strength, and your confidence to go beyond socially prescribed roles. And all this stress takes a heavy toll on your body and your mind, putting you at high risk for burnout.

Why on earth would anyone do this to herself? It sounds crazy, right? Yeah, well, so does jumping out of airplanes or kayaking down raging rapids . . . to most people.

High-achieving women do what they do because it's a challenge. It's exhilarating. It's stimulating (at least initially), and for many, it's addicting. As Brenda, a prominent criminal defense attorney, once told me, "I love my job. I love what I do. I even come to work when I'm sick. I honestly think I'd go through withdrawal if I didn't. I guess in a lot of ways I'm not a whole lot different than some of my clients. They get high on crack and I get high on work. It's my drug."

There is something to this. In the last chapter, remember when we discussed our physiological response to stress, in particular, the part about the release of adrenaline to give us that boost of energy and endorphins to increase our pain threshold? Well, those are drugs. Natural drugs, but drugs nonetheless. And when we get used to having drugs in our system and the good feelings they bring about, like strength, energy, and delay of pain, the human tendency is to want to keep those feelings pumping as much as we can—even when they may be slowly contributing to our demise.

The problem is that while our minds may want to experience this high as often and for as long as possible, our bodies simply can't do it. There isn't an unlimited supply of "happy" hormones inside of us. Our bodies need time to rest, replenish, and pay a little attention to the other systems that get neglected while we're "rushing."

But the high isn't just physical; there also is a strong psychological component to it. It's what Debbie Mandel, author of *Addicted to Stress*, calls the "'look what I can do' syndrome." "You're so productive," says Mandel. "You do it all, get it all—mother, wife, worker, with boundless energy 24/7."[1] Being all these things to all the people in your life brings about praise, internal and external rewards, admiration from others at the amazing feats you're able to accomplish, and just a generally good feeling about yourself.

There is nothing wrong with having these feelings and being proud of your accomplishments. You *are* amazing! But it's important that you understand that the rush you experience from these feelings is part of why you do what you do. And why you might not be so eager to give your poor, worn-out, depleted body a break.

It's why many high-achieving women are running on empty.

OUT OF GAS

The term *burnout* has become so familiar that it's very common to hear people casually say, "Oh, I'm so burned out," when they're referring to a bad day or a bad week. But for those who truly are out of gas, burnout is much more than a bad day or a bad week—it's a problem that significantly interferes with their health, happiness, and overall quality of life.

Interestingly, burnout isn't a medical or psychiatric diagnosis—at least not yet. But most medical and mental health professionals are familiar with the signs and symptoms of burnout. The problem is that few burnout victims seek professional help. In some cases, it's because they feel too exhausted to do anything beyond what they absolutely have to do each day. In other cases, it's because they feel ashamed, as if they have failed their families and themselves by not being stronger, by not being able to keep up or keep going. Sometimes it's both. But the reality is that if you're burned out and you don't do anything about it, your body is eventually going to do it for you. Your engine will simply stop. And unfortunately, this doesn't just mean a psychological stop. Burnout can actually lead to physical collapse and, in some cases, to death.

Fortunately, it doesn't have to get to that point. If you know what burnout looks like and you identify it early enough (meaning before you collapse and die), you can reverse it.

SIGNS OF BURNOUT

If you recall from the introduction, *burnout* is defined as a state of chronic stress and frustration that leads to:

- physical and emotional exhaustion,
- feelings of cynicism and detachment, and
- a sense of ineffectiveness and lack of accomplishment.

Together, these symptoms result in an inability to successfully function on a personal and professional level.

Each of these three areas is characterized by certain signs and symptoms, although some symptoms overlap. As we explore these areas, you'll see that many of the signs and symptoms are the same or similar to the signs of stress described in the last chapter. This is because, as with many of the concepts described in this book, the symptoms of burnout exist along a continuum. The difference between stress and burnout is often a matter of degree. Therefore, the best way to prevent burnout is to identify the symptoms as soon as possible, because the less severe the symptoms are, the easier it is to find ways to relieve them.

Signs Associated with Physical and Emotional Exhaustion

Chronic Fatigue: In the early stages of burnout, chronic fatigue is characterized by lack of energy and feeling tired most days, if not every day. You might go to bed early but wake up the next morning still feeling tired. You tend to move more slowly and find you need extra time to get ready and get out the door. At its worse, the fatigue becomes a physical and psychological state of exhaustion. You feel drained. Everything takes a concerted effort. You have no energy, so you do as little as possible to make it through the day. You find it difficult to get out of bed in the morning and might even call in sick on the days you feel like you simply can't get out of bed. This type of extreme fatigue also often results in a sense of dread for what lies ahead of you on any given day.

Insomnia: In the early stages of burnout, insomnia may be a problem only one or two nights each week. Although you feel tired, it's difficult to fall asleep; or if you do fall asleep, it's disturbed sleep; or you wake up in the middle of the night or earlier than you have to. Often, this trouble sleeping relates to persistent thoughts about the insurmountable amount of work that you have to do and whether you will be able to get it done. In the later stages, insomnia may become a nightly ordeal. As exhausted as you feel, there may be nights that you can't sleep at all.

Forgetfulness or Impaired Concentration and Attention: Physical and mental exhaustion lead to a host of cognitive problems, the most common being concentration and attention difficulties and forgetfulness. You may find yourself rereading something over and over or asking colleagues to repeat themselves. Because you can't focus, it seems to take longer to get your work done, so things begin to pile up, causing more stress. At their worst, these symptoms prevent you from getting anything done, and pretty soon, you simply can't keep up.

Physical Symptoms: All serious physical symptoms, especially chest pains or difficulty breathing, should be evaluated by a physician to rule out any medical explanations. But it's not uncommon to find that most of the physical symptoms experienced by burnout victims are caused by stress. These symptoms can include chest pains, heart palpitations, dizziness, fainting, tension headaches, migraine headaches, shortness of breath, and stomach pain. These symptoms can significantly interfere with your day-to-day functioning, making it difficult to go to work or get work done when you're there. You should also keep in mind that although there might not be a medical explanation for these symptoms at first, chronic stress can eventually lead to serious medical problems, such as heart disease, diabetes, and high blood pressure. So, if physical symptoms persist, they should be medically reevaluated from time to time.

Increased Illness: Because your body is depleted and in a weakened state, you're more vulnerable to infections, colds, flu, and other immune system disorders. The worse the burnout is, the more vulnerable you're likely to be and the longer it's likely to take you to recover from minor illnesses, like a common cold.

Loss of Appetite: In the early stages of burnout, you may not always feel hungry and may skip meals as a result. In the later stages, the situation may worsen to the point where you experience a complete loss of appetite and significant weight loss, which could be dangerous to your health.

Anxiety: Chronic anxiety is common to cases of burnout. Early in the process, the anxiety may be experienced as ongoing feelings of tension, worry, and feeling on edge. These symptoms may interfere with your ability to concentrate and attend to matters at hand. Physical symptoms might include a pounding heart or tightness in your muscles. Over time, the anxiety may become so severe that it interferes with your ability to go to work or to take care of your responsibilities at home. Feelings of apprehension and dread are common. In some cases, the anxiety may become so severe that it results in panic attacks.

Depression: As noted in the previous chapter, feeling down from time to time is normal, but in cases of burnout, depression is more than just temporary sadness. You often feel sad and hopeless. You may feel like you have no energy or you may feel irritable and restless (a form of depression called agitated depression). Guilt and feelings of worthlessness are common. You may have trouble focusing and concentrating. In depression's most severe form, you may feel trapped or think the world would be better off without you. At times, you may become preoccupied with death or dying, or have thoughts of suicide. Obviously, if the depression gets to the point where you're thinking of harming yourself, you should seek professional help immediately.

Anger: As a burnout victim, you may feel like a failure and experience a great deal of guilt. These feelings can turn into anger and resentment as the stress continues and you feel as if you have no control over it. At first, the anger may take the form of interpersonal tension with colleagues, family, or friends. As burnout becomes more severe, the anger may intensify and result in angry outbursts and serious arguments at home and in the workplace. You may have thoughts of violence toward coworkers or family, and at its most extreme, these thoughts may cross the line into actual workplace or domestic violence. If your anger gets to the point where you start thinking of hurting someone else or if you cross the line and actually get into a physical altercation, you should seek professional assistance immediately.

Signs Associated with Feelings of Detachment and Cynicism

Loss of Enjoyment: In the early stages of burnout, the loss of enjoyment you feel may be related only to work. You don't enjoy going, and when you get there, you can't wait to leave. As stress increases, the loss of enjoyment may extend to all areas of your life, including the time you spend with family and friends. At work, you may become preoccupied with thoughts of how you can avoid projects or how you can escape work altogether.

Pessimism: Burnout makes you feel like nothing is going to turn out well. While you may once have been the type of person who sees the glass as "half-full," burnout may cause you to feel as if the glass is "half-empty" or, in some cases, completely empty. This type of negativity is likely to result in negative self-talk, whereby you tell yourself, for example, that you are worthless or that you can't do anything right. These negative feelings may also carry over to how you perceive other people, causing you to feel as if no one cares or that everyone is out for themselves. This may lead to a lack of trust in coworkers, family, and friends, which in turn may increase tension at home and in the workplace and separate you from social support sources that once may have served as a buffer to your stress.

Isolation: Isolation may start out as just a mild resistance to socializing. For example, you may not feel like going to lunch with a coworker or friend, but you end up doing it anyway. As burnout worsens, you may begin to feel more and more like being alone. Colleagues dropping by to say hello may become annoying to you, and you may find yourself closing your door to keep people out. You make excuses not to go out to lunch. You search for ways to get out of meetings. In the most severe cases, you may get angry just because people speak to you. You may start locking your door to keep people away or come in early or leave late to avoid interactions with colleagues and possibly even family members.

Detachment: In burnout, detachment is a general sense of feeling disconnected from people and from your environment, and it can take the form of the isolative behaviors described above. In some situations, being detached may come across as anger toward others, but it can also take the form of removing yourself emotionally and physically from your job and your responsibilities. For example, you may start calling in sick more often or you may start missing appointments, being chronically late, or stop returning calls or e-mails.

Signs Associated with a Sense of Ineffectiveness and Lack of Accomplishment

Feelings of Apathy, Helplessness, and Hopelessness: In the beginning stages of burnout, you're likely to experience feelings of apathy, helplessness, and hopelessness, and you may have the sense that nothing is going right. As time goes on, these feelings may become immobilizing, making it seem as if nothing is worth doing, as if there is no point in even getting out of bed.

Increased Irritability: In cases of burnout, irritability is often the result of frustration over feeling ineffective and useless, as well as being disappointed over decreased productivity, worsening performance, and the dawning realization that you're not able to do things like you used to do them. You may snap at people and overreact to what in the larger scheme of things is rather trivial. In the early stages, irritability may create a rift in professional and personal relationships. In later stages, if the irritability grows into anger, it may completely destroy a career, as well as significant relationships.

Lack of Productivity and Poor Performance: Despite the fact that you continue to work long hours, the symptoms of burnout prevent you from producing the way you used to, which results in numerous incomplete projects and a stack of work that just keeps piling up. It often seems like the harder you work, the more ground you lose. And, try as you might, you just can't climb out from under the pile.

In short, burnout can take away life as you know it or once knew it. It can cause you to lose your job, your family, your friends, your sense of worth, and your identity. If you're on that path, you need to recognize the symptoms, so you can do something about them.

AM I BURNED OUT?

Based on the above descriptions of symptoms, you should have a pretty good sense of whether or not you're burned out, and, if you are, how severe your case is. If, however, you are not sure if you suffer from burnout, there are some "tests" you can do.

The first test is to leave work on a Friday and commit to treating yourself to a relaxing, stress-free weekend (or to any two consecutive days off). Although relaxing can take on many forms, for the purposes of this exercise (and for what I suspect your level of exhaustion is if you've decided to do this exercise), let's keep to a traditional relaxing, stress-free weekend. You cannot bring any work home. You can't take any work-related calls or respond to any work-related e-mails or texts or any other new methods of communication the techies may develop. If your family is a source of stress, try to get away from them for the weekend. Basically, your "job" is to remove as many sources of stress from your life as possible and infuse as many stress-reducing elements (mostly in the form of rest) into your life for two and a half days.

Try to sleep in both days. Eat right. Occupy your time with relaxing activities that you rarely allow yourself to enjoy. If you like to read, read. If you like to cook, cook. If you like to write, write. If you don't like to do anything, don't do anything. Just don't expose yourself to any stress for two and a half days.

If you awaken on Monday morning feeling tired and dreading your day, you are very likely suffering from burnout. If you want to determine the severity of your burnout, you can take a second test. But first, take a deep breath and remember to exhale, because it's going to involve your taking some of that vacation time you've probably resisted using all these years.

So here's the test. Take two weeks off from work to see if you can recover any of your strength and vitality. The same rules apply as for the first test. Remove stressors. Add stress reducers. Have fun. The whole nine yards for the entire two weeks. Because it's two weeks, and I don't want you pulling your hair out over a two-week period, you don't have to stick with the traditional stress relievers. You can try a few of the high-octane stress relievers described in chapter 8. But don't do anything too physically exhausting. Try to get at least eight hours of sleep each night and to eat at least three meals a day, preferably healthy ones.

After two weeks, if you don't feel like you've recovered very much, your problems are very likely severe and you should consider making some significant changes in your lifestyle in order to return to a normal level of functioning.[2]

REDISCOVERY

If the tests didn't turn out the way you were hoping, it's normal to feel upset. No one likes to hear that she's burned out. But the good news is that burnout isn't a terminal illness. There are things you can do to make changes, things that we'll go over in the next section. The important thing to keep in mind is that you are still the same person you were when you entered the race, maybe a little wiser to the not-always-so-pleasant ways of the world, maybe a little older. But at your core, you are the same. Your drive, your enthusiasm, your passion, and your energy may have gotten buried under the weight of the stress you've been carrying around, but those qualities and all the other good ones are still inside you. You just need to find ways to reach inside and find the sparks that first ignited your engine so that you can climb back into the driver's seat and reenter the race. You need to think about going in a new direction, and the next two chapters will provide you with a road map so that you can begin plotting your path to rediscovery.

PART THREE:
GO

Chapter 8

REFUELING:
Finding Stress Relief That Works for You

Refuel: *to supply with fresh fuel.*
—from TheFreeDictionary.com

There is simply no way to get through a long, grueling race without refueling. But as a high-achieving woman, time and time again, you push the limits until your gas tank is dangerously low. This isn't surprising. Your tendency is to push the limits on everything you do. But if you want relief from the stress that has been accumulating over the last few years (possibly even decades), then you need to refuel.

But the manner in which you decide to refuel has to be as unique as you are. There is no one-size-fits-all solution, no thirty-day program, no workshop that you can just jump into, because none of these things can possibly take into consideration all your specific circumstances. It would be easier if this weren't the case, but your life isn't easy, and a plan to relieve stress in a life as challenging as yours may be a little daunting at first. But by using everything we've discussed so far, I think it's a challenge you're ready to take on.

My job is to give you a road map that will provide you with an array of options that are available to you on your journey toward relieving stress. Your job is to consider all these options and set the course that best fits you and your individual needs. I've broken down the options into three categories: Basic Maintenance, Regular Unleaded, and High-Octane. But keep in mind that not every option will be the right fuel for your engine. In fact, when we started out, I said that many high-achieving women don't respond well to traditional stress-management strategies. These strategies work for some but not for others. That's why you need to set your own course, picking and choosing among the options that best fit with your personality, your lifestyle, and your stress level.

BASIC MAINTENANCE

If high-achieving women have one overall weakness, it's attending to basic maintenance. The warning signals are flashing brightly inside the car, but you're moving way too fast to see them. It's denial to the umpteenth degree. So let's start by working on that denial.

In the game of life, there are some basic rules that we all have to abide by. Of course, as is true for any game, you can bend the rules a little, cheat at times. But in the end, whether or not you like the rules, if you want to live, you have to find a way to work them into your life. In no particular order, these rules are:

1. You have to sleep.
2. You have to eat.
3. You have to drink.

(Of course, breathing is a rule, too. But except in worst-case scenarios, breathing is automatic.)

Due to the demands in the lives of high-achieving women, there is often a lot of cheating that goes on in the basic maintenance game. But, as you likely realize by now, you're only cheating yourself, and the cheating can have some pretty severe consequences. Without sleep, food, and water, your body won't have enough resources to replenish itself. So when you're putting together the itinerary that's going to lead you to a less stressed life, my strong recommendation is to incorporate a healthy dose of all three.

Sleep

If you recall, a survey conducted by the National Sleep Foundation (NSF) found that over two-thirds of women associate their sleep problems with stress. Yet, when pressed for time, over half of the women polled said that sleep is the first thing they give up.[1] This is an unfortunate example of short-term gain, long-term pain.

Stress leads to loss of sleep, and loss of sleep leads to an increase in stress, which becomes a vicious cycle. Sleep is a basic human need, and when we don't get enough of it, just about every aspect of our functioning is affected. We move slower. We're less productive. We're more irritable. We make poor decisions. We forget things. And all these problems are exacerbated as you lose more and more sleep.

Excessive sleep loss has been linked to mood disorders, heart disease, diabetes, high blood pressure, substance abuse, obesity, impaired judgment, reckless behavior, and increased accidents at home, at work, and on the road.[2] In fact, in the most severe cases of sleep deprivation, hallucinations and paranoid delusions can develop. The worst-case scenario is death.

I'm not trying to scare you—although if that's what it takes, I'm not opposed to it. I just want to break down some of the denial I commonly see in high-achieving women. The truth is that loss of sleep leads to all the things you're stressing out about, so if something has to get bumped from your to-do list, you should strongly consider that it *not* be sleep.

Why is sleep so important? Because it's the only block of time in your hectic life that your body has a chance to recharge. Although your body is resting (hopefully) while you sleep, your brain isn't. It's actually very active. Sleep is the time when your body and brain replenish themselves. This is accomplished through what sleep experts call our "sleep architecture," a relatively predictable pattern that occurs in ninety-minute cycles while we sleep. It involves an alternating pattern of rapid eye movement (REM) sleep and non-REM sleep.[3]

According to the NSF, "REM sleep is an active sleep where dreams occur, breathing and heart rate increase and become irregular, muscles relax and eyes move back and forth under the eyelids."[4] It's characterized by a high level of mental and physical activity during which your heart rate, blood pressure, and breathing are very similar to what they are like when you're awake. REM sleep accounts for about 25 percent of our sleep time, and it first occurs about ninety minutes after you fall asleep. It is the REM stage of sleep that provides energy to your brain and body and that helps you perform throughout the day.[5]

The other 75 percent of our sleep time is spent in non-REM sleep. Non-REM sleep has four distinct stages. Stage 1 is the beginning stage of drowsiness just as you're starting to doze off. Stage 2 represents the onset of actual sleep. Breathing and heart rate remain regular, and body temperature drops. In stages 3 and 4, your blood pressure lowers, muscles relax, and breathing slows down. Stages 3 and 4 are the deepest stages of sleep and provide your body with the best chance to restore what you used up during the daytime.[6]

Sleep experts believe that the best sleep involves the right combination of REM and non-REM sleep. But how much is enough? Most sleep guidelines indicate that adults should get between seven and nine hours of sleep each night for optimum performance, health, and safety. However, as with most things, there isn't a magic number. Different people need different amounts of sleep, and these needs actually change at different stages of life. Babies need a lot of sleep. Adults need less, but they still need enough for healthy aging and functioning. Some adults might feel perfectly fine with seven hours of sleep, while others may need ten.

So how can you figure out how much sleep you need? Sleep experts recommend that you take a look at your individual lifestyle, needs, and habits. You should know by now how you react to different amounts of sleep. How are your mood, concentration, and energy level after six hours of sleep? After eight hours of sleep? Determining how each these areas is affected is often a good indication of how much sleep is best for you.

However, it's not always that simple. The NSF reports that the amount of sleep a person needs is influenced by two factors. One is what researchers call a person's basal sleep need, which is the amount of sleep your body needs on a regular basis for optimal performance. The other is called sleep debt. Sleep debt is defined as the accumulated sleep that is lost over time, due to poor sleep habits, sickness, insomnia, or any other environmental factors that prevent sleep.[7]

Studies have found that although most adults have a basal sleep need of seven to eight hours a night, things gets a bit complicated when sleep debt is entered into the equation. For example, even if you get seven or eight hours of sleep a few nights in a row, your sleep debt from previous nights of sleep loss may still cause you to feel sleepy and inattentive.[8] The key is to get as much basal sleep and accumulate as little sleep debt as possible. Not easy in a world that never seems to sleep, but there are ways to get the most out of whatever sleep time you can squeeze into your busy life.

One of the most important things you can do is to keep a consistent sleep/wake schedule, including on your days off. Even if you can get only six hours of sleep each night, make sure you go to bed around the same time and wake up around the same time seven days a week. A lot of people stay up late on their days off because they don't have to wake up early for work. But this is a sure way to throw off your sleep cycle, making you feel tired when you have to start on a different sleep/wake schedule on your next day back to work.

It's also a good idea to develop a relaxing bedtime routine, starting about an hour (or more) before you plan to go to bed. You shouldn't rush around or do physical exercise during that time. In fact, if you're going to exercise, you should try to do it at least a few hours before bedtime. You also shouldn't watch thrillers or read scary books right before bed. In other words, you shouldn't do anything to get your adrenaline pumping right before you go to bed because it takes time for your body to settle down.

Also try not to eat right before bed, and avoid caffeine, alcohol, and tobacco several hours before bedtime. Caffeine and tobacco keep you awake. Alcohol interferes with REM sleep.

Because light inhibits sleep, you should keep your bedroom as dark as possible. You also want to make the bedroom a place that you associate with sleep. You don't want to work on your computer or watch television in your bedroom. Both of these activities have been found to hinder sleep. So use your computer and watch TV in another room, so that your brain starts to associate your bedroom with sleep, not work. The basic idea is to do things that promote sleep and to avoid things that interfere with sleep in the hours before bedtime.

If only it were that easy, right? Stress, as you know, is a leading cause of sleep problems. Worries related to work, marriage, children, and any other stressful experiences that intrude in our day-to-day lives are going to interfere in our ability to get good sleep. That's why insomnia is one of the most common symptoms reported by high-achieving women.

Your mind races, new and exciting ideas pop into your head at night when you're trying to settle into sleep—or worse, worries that you can't shake keep rearing their heads. All these problems not only can make it difficult to fall asleep (most people's definition of insomnia), but also they can cause you to wake up in the middle of the night, to wake up earlier than you need to, or they can disturb your sleep so that you don't feel rested when you wake up (all three of which are also forms of insomnia).

If insomnia is a persistent problem, you should see a doctor to rule out any medical causes. If there are none (or even if there are), you can try deep breathing, imagery, or even counting sheep to help you sleep. But if after twenty minutes or so you're still awake, it serves no purpose to just lie there, watching the clock, frustrated that you can't get the sleep you so desperately need. In fact, it's counterproductive.

So what's the solution? Most sleep experts recommend that you get out of bed, move to a different room, and do something calming, like reading or listening to relaxing music. I personally recommend doing something incredibly boring, maybe something you keep putting off doing because it is so boring. But whatever you choose, it shouldn't be anything that stimulates your brain. Then, when you feel sleepy, go back to bed and try again.

The key is to treat sleep as important as anything else you do. In fact, you may find it helpful to actually write sleep into your schedule—the way you schedule anything else that's important in your life.

Eating

Just like sleep, healthful eating helps to restore your body's balance. It's also what literally keeps you going by giving your cells the fuel (calories) they need to keep all your systems working properly. While there is no consensus on whether eating three meals a day or the newer trend of six smaller meals a day is best, there is clear agreement that skipping meals is not good for your health.

But it's not just about eating. It's about eating right. Although I think most would agree that eating something is better than eating nothing at all, healthful eating is important to overall health and stress levels.

Diet is a personal decision and is influenced by a lot of factors, so I'm not going to get into what you should and shouldn't eat. If you're interested in learning more about healthful eating, many resources exist. One such resource can be found at the Harvard School of Public Health (HSPH) (http://www.hsph.harvard.edu/), which features a diagram called the Healthy Eating Pyramid to help consumers make healthful food choices. But most of you know that, when it comes to eating, the best choices are plant-based foods, which include vegetables, fruits, and whole grains. And if you eat meat, then poultry and fish are the best options. Unsurprisingly, the less healthful choices are red meat, refined grains, starches, sugar, and salty snacks.

Of course, one of the biggest problems for high-achieving women is time—or lack thereof. That's why many of you have made fast-food restaurants one of your favorite pit stops as you drive to and from all the places life takes you. But as you may have noticed, fast-food restaurants don't offer much in the way of vegetables, fruits, whole grains, or fish (although some are making improvements to their menus). Therefore, the habit of driving through fast-food lines to get some calories into your food-deprived body isn't the best option, which I suspect you already know.

So what is the best option for busy women? I recommend that you adjust your schedule to make time for healthful and nutritious meals. Not only does it give your body the fuel it needs to recharge, it also gives your brain some downtime, hopefully away from work. (I suspect you know this, as well, but you probably don't always apply it, which is why we're going over basic maintenance in the first place.)

What about eating lunch at work? I'd say if it's a matter of eating at work or not eating at all, I'd go with the eating-at-work option. But again, the best way to reduce stress on your body and mind is to get out and enjoy a healthful meal. When you return to work, you'll probably be much more productive.

Drinking

Drinking has become a bad habit for most Americans—and I'm not just talking about alcohol. There are so many options today when it comes to selecting something to drink, and, as it turns out, most of the choices we make are not the healthiest. According to Dr. Barry Popkin, a leading scholar on dietary patterns, the trend among all age groups is toward high-calorie sweetened drinks.[9] But even those who try to make healthful choices are often confused by misleading advertising and deceptive labels telling consumers what's "healthy."

For example, you might think a cranberry juice cocktail is healthy because its name contains the word *cranberry*. After all, cranberry is a fruit, and fruit is good for us, right? But according to the Nutrition Source and the Department of Nutrition at the Harvard School of Public Health, a twelve-ounce serving of cranberry juice cocktail contains the equivalent of twelve teaspoons of sugar. And many fruit smoothies are even worse, with some having upward of the equivalent of fifteen teaspoons of sugar in every twelve-ounce serving.[10] That's not to say that sodas are healthful in comparison. Their sugar equivalents average around eleven teaspoons per twelve-ounce serving. Then, of course, there's the debate over whether milk and fruit juice are good for us.

This confusion over what is and isn't healthful prompted an independent group of nutrition experts to establish the Beverage Guidance Panel.[11] The panel offers recommendations on the best range of intake for each of the six groups of beverages. The clear winner is water. The suggested amount is sixteen to twenty-four or more ounces daily (although it's not possible to establish a set amount of water necessary for every person, since water needs depend partially on overall diet and the amount of water in the food consumed). Without enough water, our bodies become dehydrated, which can lead to an increased risk for colon and bladder diseases. But water isn't the only beverage recommended by the panel. Unsweetened coffee and tea come in second place after water, with a recommendation of up to eight daily servings of tea and four servings of coffee. Next is nonfat or low-fat milk and fortified soy beverages of up to two servings daily followed by diet drinks and fruit juices. In last place are soft drinks.[12]

What about alcohol? That's a touchy subject. Some experts say that moderate alcohol consumption lowers the risk for heart disease and diabetes, but some say it increases the risk for breast and colon cancer. For pregnant women, it's obviously a no-no. The same applies for those with substance abuse problems, liver disease, or anyone who takes medication that adversely interacts with alcohol. We also know that alcohol is a central nervous system depressant, so it is not a good choice for stressed-out, depressed people. And we know that alcohol interferes with sleep, which, for a mostly sleep-deprived population, isn't good either. Although consuming alcohol is a personal decision, for high-achieving women who are stressed out, it's my opinion that the costs outweigh the benefits.

The best thing you can do for your body is to drink water throughout the day. Keep caffeinated drinks under control. And try to stay away from the sweetened soft drinks.

REGULAR UNLEADED

In this section, we'll cover the more traditional stress-management strategies. As I've said before, these strategies don't always fit well into the lives of high-achieving women; in fact, there simply may not be enough time in your life to do some of these things, at least not as often as they're recommended. But if time is the only issue, you should at least try to fit some of these strategies into your day, even if they're mini versions.

On the other hand, if you're like many high-achieving women who find many of the traditional stress-management strategies to be counterproductive, then you shouldn't try to force something into your stress-management plan that doesn't work for you. I know some high-achieving women who would rather beat their heads against the wall than sit through a yoga class. "It just stresses me out," they say. And that's okay. If something mentioned in this section works, then use it. If not, ignore it. Again, it's your course to plot. The goal is to discover a routine that works for you, so let's see what options traditional stress management has to offer.

Balance

I'm going to say right up front that I have an issue with the whole "balance" movement. Don't get me wrong—there is absolutely nothing wrong with balancing the various parts of your life. In fact, if you can achieve it, or even some semblance of it, balance away!

But the balance movement, in my experience, has done a real number on high-achieving women, and not in a good way. What do high-achieving women strive for? Achievement, right? Yet true balance, in today's world, is unachievable unless you're one of the rare individuals who can do whatever she wants whenever she wants. And I don't know anyone like that.

Because high-achieving women are who they are, many of them have taken on this whole balance thing as if it's a challenge they need to accomplish, and that leads to more unnecessary stress. So you need to ask yourself, how much additional stress are you taking on by attempting to capture this elusive balance that everyone seems to be talking about, but no one ever seems to have?

There should be no stress in balance. Stress and balance are supposed to be on opposite ends of the continuum. But high-achieving women are . . . well, just so darn high-achieving! They are perfectionistic, competitive, assertive—all qualities that are, within reason, okay. But if you're going to strive for balance, you can't take it on as a mission you have to tackle and conquer every day, creating a perfectly balanced scale where everyone in your life is happy because you devoted just the right amount of time to each of them. If you think in terms of the end result instead of the process, you're going to be disappointed. And you're going to get all stressed out over balance, which is just silly. So if you want to go for balance, here's what I recommend. Adjust your thinking. Don't view it in terms of all-or-none. Get whatever balance you can get in your life and be happy about it.

You also have to decide what the right balance is for you. Who said that balance had to be 50/50, with half of your life devoted to work and the other half to home and family? No one. If 50/50 is best for you, try to get as close to it as possible, knowing that you won't succeed all the time or maybe any of the time. In fact, some days, you may not even come close. But you're doing the best you can, and you should reward yourself for the effort. If 75/25 fits better in your world, then that's what you should strive for.

Don't let balance define you. You define balance based on who you are, how you live, and what you want. I suggest looking at it the same way you might look at becoming a billionaire. Most of us would like to achieve that status, but the reality is that very few of us ever will. Well, the same holds true for "work/life balance." There's nothing wrong with having it as a goal; it's a healthy goal to strive for. But if you're not realistic about it, it will turn into an unhealthy goal and only add to your stress.

My advice is to try not to squeeze your uniquely shaped peg into what unfortunately has become a one-size-fits-all hole that we've come to refer to as work/life balance. Balance is self-defined; it's what works for you and your family. If you allow it to be anything else, you're only adding another thing to your to-do list, and I think that list is long enough, don't you?

Discover or Rediscover Ways to Relax

Busy schedules have a way of eliminating activities you may once have found relaxing. So many high-achieving women have drifted so far away from anything resembling relaxation that they often tell me they can't think of any relaxing activities. I say, try. At some point in your life, you must have done some things that relaxed you. Try to remember what those things were and see if you can find ways to incorporate them into your life.

Journaling

For some women, "journaling"—writing your thoughts and feelings down on paper—is a powerful stress reliever. A friend describes it as "lifting a heavy weight out of my head and off of my shoulders." A similar activity that works for some women is to keep a pencil and paper by their bedside. Then, when a thought or idea pops into their mind at bedtime, they can write it down to get it out of their mind and onto the paper. If you try this method, I recommend you use a large tablet so that if you get an idea after you've turned out the light, you can just scribble the note in the dark, without worrying about writing over words or off the page. Turning on the light each time you get an idea is likely to interfere with your ability to get to sleep quickly.

Exercise

I know! Exercise. Who has time for it? But exercise can be a great stress reducer and it also promotes health and weight control, so if you can find a way to fit it in, do it. The Centers for Disease Control and Prevention (CDC) recommend that you do two types of physical activity each week to improve your health and reduce stress: aerobic activity and muscle strengthening. In order to achieve important health benefits from exercise, adults need at least 2.5 hours each week of moderate-intensity aerobic exercise, such as brisk walking, or 1.25 hours of vigorous aerobic activity, like jogging,[13] as well as twice-a-week or more sessions of strengthening exercises that work all major muscle groups.

With your busy schedules, I'm sure many of you are thinking, "Dream on." But if you can't find the time for a complete exercise routine, you can still incorporate exercise into your day whenever possible. For example, you can take a brisk ten-minute walk during your lunch hour or before or after work, park your car far from your building so you have to walk, or take the stairs instead of the elevator.

You can also get creative in the ways you incorporate fitness into your daily routine. A friend of mine, whose commute to work leaves her stuck in traffic up to an hour each way, keeps light-weight dumbbells on the passenger seat of her car. While she's sitting in traffic, she does a mini arm workout in her car. Another friend, who is a writer, prints out her manuscripts and walks around her house or around the neighborhood on a nice day with pen and manuscript in hand, editing as she goes, instead of sitting idly at her desk.

There are also exercises you can do right at your desk. For example, try rolling your wrists, ankles, neck, and shoulders while you're working at your desk. Not only does this keep your blood circulating, it can also be relaxing. You can also stretch your muscles by turning your torso from side to side, reaching up or to the side with your arms, and flexing your calves. For a mini abdominal workout, tighten your stomach muscles, hold the contraction for a few seconds, then release; you can do the same with your buttock muscles. You can even do Kegel exercises at your desk.

Another good seated exercise is calf raises. Put your feet flat on the floor, then pull your heels up so the weight goes to the balls of your feet, using your own muscles as resistance. For even more resistance, use your hands to push down on your knees as you're lifting your heels. And don't forget about deep breathing—another calming activity that is easy to do while you're sitting.

So no more excuses that you don't have time to exercise. If you don't have time to add a full workout into your schedule, find creative ways to fit exercise into your daily routine. In addition to its stress-reducing qualities, exercise is good for your physical and mental health, weight, and overall well-being.

Use Imagery

The idea behind imagery is simple: close your eyes and use your imagination to take you to a relaxing place in your mind, and your body will follow. The basic idea is to build a mental collection of relaxing images or experiences that are readily available to you when you need them. When you're feeling stressed (or to relax even further), go to that collection of soothing images in your mind and pull one out. Close your eyes and mentally take yourself to the place in the image.

The more senses you bring into the experience, the more relaxing the experience should be. So, for example, if you're imagining yourself at a beach, bring into that experience the sound of the waves rhythmically rolling onto the beach, the smell of the salt air, and the feeling of warmth from the sun. By using as many senses as possible, your relaxation should be even further enhanced. Using deep breathing and imagery together can be even more effective.

The possibilities of imagined scenes and events are infinite and unique to who you are and to what you find relaxing. If the beach doesn't work for you, imagine a mountain scene or any experience in your life that brought you joy or good feelings. Some people don't use actual scenes or past events at all; they create their own images, such as thinking of themselves as being light as a feather, gliding through the air. Others visualize their stress escaping, melting, or flowing out of their bodies. Some imagine taking their worries and locking them up in a box or throwing them away. Again, the point is to find what works best for you and to use it when you feel stressed.

Prioritize

When you prioritize, you can manage your time more effectively. In every schedule, some things are more important to do than others. By prioritizing what has to be handled immediately and what can wait for later in the day, week, month, or year, you can reduce your stress and better manage your time. To help you prioritize, use the written to-do lists we've previously discussed.

Schedule Nonnegotiable Blocks for "You Time"

Schedule blocks of time in your planner for you to do things unrelated to work. And try not to unschedule them for something else. Just use the time to focus on yourself.

Take a Break

Walk away from your work for a few minutes (every hour or two, if you can). It doesn't have to be a long break; the purpose is just to clear your brain. The key, however, is to not get pulled into something else during the break. Taking a moment to clear your mind is very different than getting distracted by other work, by questions from coworkers, or by any of the other kinds of interruptions that frequently occur in the workplace. It also helps if you leave your work marked in some kind of way so that when you return after a few minutes of brain clearing, you can more easily pick up where you left off.

Reframe

There are so many ways to view the same situation, so why not try to see something in a positive light rather than a negative light? One way to do this is to ask yourself what positives could come out of this experience. Another way is to think of difficult and challenging situations as unique opportunities for growth. Don't turn every situation into a catastrophe. Few experiences at work would qualify as true catastrophes, yet we often think of them as such. Reframe challenging experiences as interesting problems that need innovative solutions, and act calmly to figure out the best solutions.

You can also use reframing to understand other people's behavior. If you find yourself upset or stressed over something someone said to you or over the way someone treated you, ask yourself why it might have happened. And don't stop at "She's a demon from hell who has always hated me and lives to make my life miserable." The point of this exercise is not to justify or excuse others for behaving badly or to allow them to abuse you but rather to consider alternative explanations that might help you interpret their intentions differently. Allowing yourself to step out of the experience and consider it from another perspective not only may reduce the stress you feel over the situation but also may keep you from acting rashly on perceptions that aren't necessarily accurate.

Surround Yourself with Positive People

In the workplace and in life in general, it's easy to spot positive and negative people. Positive people usually have a lot of energy, and their energy and enthusiastic spirits often serve to lift the spirits of others. Negative people tend to do the opposite. They frequently complain. They rarely, if ever, have a good thing to say about anyone or anything, and they often engage in mean-spirited gossip that drains the energy and spirit of everyone involved. This is why it's extremely difficult to stay positive around negative people.

If you want to stay positive, hang around as many positive people as possible and remove as many negative people as possible from your life. If there are negative people in your life that you can't escape, try to keep their negativity from pulling you down to their level. One strategy you can try is to change the subject whenever a conversation veers off into negativity. If that doesn't work, simply walk away. If you can't walk away, try responding to the negative statements with positive ones. And if none of these efforts work, you may want to call the person on it. In other words, you may want to point out the seemingly constant negativity and how it fuels other people's pessimism. Sometimes people aren't necessarily aware of how much negativity they exude. Simply calling attention to it may result in a change in their behavior.

Laugh

Surround yourself with people who are funny. Do things that make you laugh. Watch a comedy. Laugh at yourself once in a while. Laughter replenishes the mind and is a great way to reduce stress. It may even be good for your health. A study out of the University of Maryland found that laughter and a good sense of humor may prevent heart disease and reduce the risk of heart attack. The results found that people with heart disease were 40 percent less likely to laugh in a variety of situations compared with people in the same age range who did not have heart disease.[14]

Consider Same-Career Couple Opportunities

Although this certainly won't work for everyone, if you're happily married and if working together is a possibility, you may want to consider it. I know it sounds crazy. In fact, some people say that the fastest way to divorce court is to work with your partner, and that may be true for some couples. However, research has found some stress-relieving benefits in same-career couples.[15]

According to researcher Jonathon Halbesleben, who has done much of the work in this area of study, the high level of integration between home/life and work among same-career couples offers them greater work-related resources. The effect seems to be lower burnout rates, higher performance levels, and higher work involvement. Halbesleben says that same-career couples perceive higher levels of social support from their partners and coworkers, which lowers their stress levels and their risk for burnout.[16] So, as crazy as it may sound, it apparently works for some.

HIGH-OCTANE

If you haven't figured it out by now, people sometimes get locked into perceptions or definitions. High-achieving women are as guilty of this as anyone else, sometimes more so. I'll give you the example of Betty, a burned-out high-achieving woman who insisted that nothing she tried relaxed her. She called herself "relax-resistant."

"I've tried a meditation class," she said. "If it wouldn't have been so embarrassing, I would have run screaming out the door in the first two minutes. Instead, I sat through it and left more stressed than when I went in. Yoga. Same thing. Day spa. Bored out of my mind. Nothing works for me."

"What about vacations?" I asked.

"I want to come home as soon as I get there. I tried lying on the beach, listening to the waves. I even had a few drinks to calm me down, and it was okay for a while. But then my mind went to this and to that. I ended up leaving earlier than my friends and coming back to work."

I asked Betty to define *vacation*, and she looked at me like I had three heads. She insisted that everyone knew what a vacation was, but I persisted, and finally she said it was a time away from work where you do something relaxing. So I asked her to define *relaxing*.

"It's when you just chill out. Don't do anything serious. Just breathe slowly and discover your inner self, I suppose."

I then asked her if that was her definition of relaxing or someone else's, since it didn't seem like chilling out, breathing slowly, and discovering her inner self was all that relaxing to her. But Betty just kept going back to "that's just what relaxing means," that's how "everybody" defines it. She even insisted that we get a dictionary and look up the word so she could prove to me that she was right.

Betty was doing what many high-achieving women do—trying to force the wrong fuel down their high-performance engines. And it just makes their engine run worse.

No one can say what is relaxing to another person; one can only say what relaxes oneself. As such, relaxing is in the mind of the relaxer. The same holds true for stress reduction. So I've put together some of the high-octane fuels I've discovered over the years from working with high achievers who eventually came to the realization that they had to think outside the box to find the right fuel for their engines. Many were resistant to the idea at first, as you may be, thinking it was too far afield from what relaxation "should be." But that's the whole point of thinking outside the box. You don't know until you give it a chance.

Now, I don't want to limit you. I want your mind to wander as far as you will allow it to go, so I'm not going to suggest *what* you should do or *how* you should do it. That kind of "do this, then do that" approach works well with traditional stress-management techniques; it doesn't work so well for high-octane solutions. But just to get the pistons going, I'll throw out a few ideas to get you started.

Extreme Vacations

Extreme vacations are made for people who love challenges, so they're often the perfect getaway for stressed-out, high-achieving women. An extreme vacation not only takes them away from the stress of the workplace, it also doesn't bore them to tears. Depending on what you're into, extreme vacations can challenge you physically, mentally, and, in some cases, both—and you can find these challenges just about anywhere in the world. For example, the Extreme Adventures Web site of Abercrombie & Kent encourages travelers to think of extreme vacations as life-changing experiences: "From the polar ice caps to the deserts of Africa and all points in between, these adventures are sure to challenge and change you."[17]

That's actually a good way to approach a getaway. After all, you live only once, and I really doubt that when you're on your last leg, you're going to say, "Gee, I wish I had spent more time in the office."[18] So think about what you would like to do—now, before you get to that point—and then do it.

Would you love to see polar bears up close and personal in the Arctic? Maybe you'd like to go dog sledding in Norway or go on a camel safari in Kenya. ShermansTravel.com offers shark diving, gorilla safaris, and more.[19] How about African safaris, running with the bulls, heli-skiing, drag racing (yes, it exists as a vacation), sand boarding in the Peruvian desert, spelunking (I'm not going to tell you, look it up yourself)? If you want to tone it down a notch, consider cycling, rock climbing, ski vacations, or sightseeing in the Grand Canyon. Just find something that you think will rejuvenate your spirit, and then go for it.

Yes, most of these vacations are expensive. But if you're like many high achievers, you haven't taken a real vacation in years. Sylvia Hewlett's survey of extreme workers found that 53 percent of those surveyed regularly gave up vacations days they were entitled to, 42 percent took ten or fewer vacation days a year, 17 percent took five or fewer vacation days a year, and 5 percent took no vacation at all.[20] Just think of all the money you should have spent on your health and well-being over the years. I'd say you're due.

Extreme Sports

Extreme sports are not for everyone, but if you're into activities that involve speed, heights, stamina, pushing your physical limits, and an element of danger, then extreme sports might be the right fuel for your engine. In some cases, extreme sports can be combined with extreme vacations, such as trips to go mountain or rock climbing, skiing, snowboarding, kayaking down the rapids, surfing, or mountain biking. But you don't necessarily have to travel to find an extreme sport. You can do some of these activities locally. Possibilities include amateur ice hockey, skydiving, bungee jumping, cycling, and skateboarding. If you live near water, how about windsurfing, waterskiing, or powerboat racing? If you live at high elevations, you might want to try hang gliding, ski jumping, or cliff diving. And if you want to tone it down, take away the "extreme" and consider a community softball, basketball, or tennis league.

Extreme Hobbies

Hobbies can be great stress relievers, but when people think of hobbies, many think of more laid-back activities, such as photography, building model airplanes, and gardening. If these kinds of hobbies work for you, that's great. But that's thinking inside the box. For those of you who have trouble with laid-back activities, you need to think outside the box—find something that fits well with your intensity and your drive, something that will ignite your passion or your competitiveness (if that's your style). Here are a few ideas: bow-and-arrow shooting, target shooting, self-defense classes, paintball, or the real killer—playing *Wii Sports* with your kids. That can really get competitive!

Extreme Workouts

Much like extreme sports, extreme workouts are not for everyone, but they certainly would qualify as "vigorous aerobics" when you're counting your weekly minutes to get the health benefits from exercise described by the CDC. If you think extreme workouts might be something you'd enjoy and can make the time for, consider spinning classes, boot camp workouts, karate, kickboxing, or shadow boxing.

Find a Cause

As Elizabeth Scott, a wellness coach who specializes in stress management, writes, "People are generally more happy when they have meaning in their lives, and part of living a meaningful life is having a feeling of making a difference in the world."[21] For most high-achieving women, much of the meaning in their lives has to do with the fulfillment they get from their work. However, that doesn't necessarily last forever, especially in cases of burnout, nor is it completely healthy or satisfying. My advice is to not put all your eggs in one basket, so to speak, when you can avoid it.

One way to diversify is to spread your passion among different activities. Get involved in a cause that you care deeply about. Whatever the cause may be—politics, global warming, rescue missions, homelessness, food banks, domestic violence shelters, food kitchens, or anything else you feel passionate about—jumping in and helping out can be a good way to relieve stress and add more balance to your life. An important caveat though: always keep in mind the basic message that there are only twenty-four hours in a day. It's great to get involved in a cause. It can reenergize you, make you feel good about yourself, and reduce stress. But if you add something to your plate, something else has to be taken off, or the result is going to be added stress rather than reduced stress in your life.

Challenge Your Brain

Few things are more exciting for high-achieving women than engaging their brains in a new challenge. But many don't think they have the time to take on anything new, or, once they're set in their professions, they simply don't think of new ways to remain intellectually challenged. Yet opportunities for mental stimulation are all around us.

What about learning a new language? Don't think you have the time? Buy CDs or audio downloads that you can listen to while driving to and from work or while traveling on a plane. If you have a family, you can make it a family learning experience during long car or plane trips. There are also thousands of audiobooks in just about every genre imaginable—fiction, business, medicine, sports, humor, inspirational, poetry, philosophy—that you can listen to while traveling on the road or in the air.

Other intellectual activities include going back to school, exploring new career opportunities, or doing crossword puzzles. If you're interested in history, consider visiting museums or beginning a collection of rare coins or stamps. If you like music, learn to play an instrument or return to an instrument you once played. Treat yourself to the opera, a symphony, or the theater.

After Burn

Just make sure you don't jump out of the frying pan and into the fire. After you've climbed your mountains and run the rapids, you still have to sleep, eat, and drink. Those are nonnegotiable. And you can't add more to your schedule until you take something off. Better time management can help you find more time, but rarely can it add so much time to your schedule that you don't have to renegotiate some of your commitments in order to add others. It's a simple matter of math.

YOU'RE NOT ORDINARY

These high-octane methods and as many more as you can imagine are certainly not the ordinary ways most people relax, but then again—you're not ordinary. Say it out loud if you have to . . . *I am not ordinary!*

You thrive on excitement. You experience things passionately. And you love challenges. So why should you limit that to your work life? Who ever said you had to? You don't have to fit your round peg into the square hole society has cut out for you. You can cut out your own space—one that fits you exactly. And the way you do this is by using the road map I've provided and by plotting your own course.

Decide how you're going to maneuver around the treacherous terrain of the workplace and the societal ties that keep you from moving forward. Figure out ways you can manage with less technology in your life. Experiment with moving up or down on the personality and communication continuums we've discussed. And, equally important, plot an effective course using the stress-management strategies that you feel most comfortable with and that work best for you. This way you'll be able to successfully manage the obstacles in your path.

By doing these things, you should find yourself leaving the dangerous road you've been traveling on—the one that leads to burnout—and crossing over to a safer and healthier road—a path that will reignite your sense of personal joy and professional fulfillment.

Chapter 9

GETTING BACK IN THE DRIVER'S SEAT:
Overcoming Burnout

Getting Back in the Driver's Seat: to return to a position of power, dominance, or control.
—from infoplease.com

S o you're burned out. You're exhausted. You feel disconnected and disenfranchised. You've lost your drive and your passion. And stress relief either hasn't helped or it hasn't helped enough to make you feel like you're back where you need to be. Something is missing.

If that's how you feel, you're right. You're burned out. But as I said before, burnout isn't a terminal condition. You can overcome it. You just have to be prepared for the fact that you're going to have to make some pretty substantial changes to life as you know it in order to effect a change in how you're feeling.

As you now know, your burnout didn't develop overnight, and it's not going to go away overnight either. Even if you took the "test" in chapter 7 and you felt better afterward, the reality is that as soon as you return to the challenging life you lead as a high-achieving woman, most if not all of that stress is still going to be there. Unless you do a good job of inoculating yourself, it will wear you down again, probably much quicker than it did the first time, because your system has been weakened by the chronic stress.

It's also important that you understand that this is going to take some time. In all the previous chapters, I've tried to suggest as many strategies as possible that don't take a lot of extra time, knowing that it's hard for you to add more to your already overflowing plate. However, burnout is different, and there are no mini stress relievers or quick solutions that are going to immediately fix it.

So, with this understanding in mind, let's get started and see if we can't get you moving again in the right direction.

167

TAKE AN INVENTORY

The first thing you should do is honestly assess and take inventory of all the situations that cause you to feel stressed, anxious, worried, frustrated, and helpless. Don't do this in your mind; you have enough going on in there already. Besides, making a list provides you with a visual reference and keeps you organized as you go through all the various aspects of your life that cause you stress.

Use the first section of this book to make sure you cover all the different areas that commonly lead to stress in the lives of high-achieving women. Be sure to consider not just the normal workplace pressures, like long hours and heavy workload, but also the gender-based stressors that will probably be harder to pinpoint because of their "invisibility." Make sure you consider social factors and technological stressors—all the things we covered earlier.

Don't rush through the list to get everything done as quickly as you can. You're not competing with anyone. It's not a race; it's a process. In fact, you should consider it a work in progress, adding things that might come to you later.

Once you have completed the list (knowing you can add to it at any time), get a notebook or some paper and make a hierarchy of the things you feel are most to least responsible for your burnout. Put only two items on a page to give yourself room to work with later on (one per page, if you like a lot of space).

Once you have the rank-ordered list, starting with the first item and moving down, try to think of ways to modify the stressor. Some may be harder than others because, as we've discussed, there are some stressors you're going to have little or no control over. But you should still try to think of at least one stress modifier for each stressor, even if it's something you have to do on your own to make a difference.

Once you've created your inventory, begin to implement the ideas you've come up with to reduce the stressors you've identified. Try not to get frustrated if you don't start to see immediate changes or to feel immediate results. Burnout is a different kind of animal, and it's likely to take some time before you notice any significant changes.

JUST SAY *NO*

While you're "recovering," don't take on any new commitments or responsibilities that you can avoid. I realize you aren't going to be able to evade all new commitments—you do have to live in the real world, and there are going to be things you just can't get out of doing. But for the reasons we went over in chapter 5, you're prone to say *yes* instead of *no* at the mere suggestion that something might need to get handled or that someone might need some help. Resist that urge.

REMEMBER THOSE LISTS

For those commitments and responsibilities you already have, make rank-ordered lists like the ones we covered in chapter 5. Get in the habit of making a daily list of the things that must be done that day and the things that can be put off to another day. Once you finish the "must do" side, do as many of the things as you can on the "can do" side, scratching off tasks as you accomplish them.

You should also make a list of "must do" and "can delegate," as suggested in chapter 5, remembering that when you delegate (and I encourage delegating as much as possible), you should try not to jump in and take back the task at the first sign of a mistake or because the "delegatee" is moving too slowly for your high-speed brain. If you take back all the delegated work, it defeats the purpose of the making the list, and the last thing you want to do with your valuable time is to waste it.

Most important, don't forget to give yourself pats on the back as you complete tasks. Reinforcement reduces stress and makes you feel good. Therefore, the kinds of rewards you give yourself should be based on what you value most, what makes you feel good.

One type of reward you can use is internal reinforcement, such as positive self-talk. Positive self-talk is any statement you make to yourself that is uplifting and intended to boost your self-esteem and self-confidence. Examples include: "I did a great job" or "I can overcome this challenge." Another example of internal reinforcement is allowing yourself to "stay in the moment" or "bask in the glow." It's basically just taking a moment to appreciate the good work you've done before you race off to start another project.

A second type of reward is external reinforcement, such as buying something you've been wanting or engaging in an activity you enjoy. This can include anything from sending yourself flowers to going roller-skating with friends. Although I don't typically encourage using food as a reward (unless you're one of the few who finds broccoli to be a rewarding snack), treating yourself to a nice dinner occasionally isn't a bad idea, especially if it's with your significant other (a date!), family, or friends.

It also is sometimes helpful to decide what your rewards will be ahead of time; that way, you'll have something to look forward to and something that may motivate you to accomplish your goals.

TAKE BREAKS BETWEEN BIG PROJECTS

While you're recovering (and really anytime, if it's possible), try to take breaks between big projects or cases. Don't jump from one stressful, time-consuming project to the next if you can avoid it. Remember that your system is in a weakened condition from the burnout, and if you keep stressing it out without a chance for it to recover, you're going to be in the same boat you were in when you started this whole process.

FORCE YOURSELF TO LEAVE

Force yourself to leave work at a reasonable hour as many days as you can. Yes, I understand the types of jobs you gravitate toward usually require long hours. But you're burned out and if you keep everything that caused you to burn out status quo, then you're going to stay burned out. It's a simple matter of choices and consequences.

If your boss isn't willing to be flexible on the hours, you may want to consider having a heart-to-heart, explaining that you're very committed to your job, but you need a little time to recharge your batteries. No one wants to admit she's burned out, but if you want to stay in the race, you have to do what you have to do.

RESIST THE URGE TO TAKE WORK HOME

I know. You have a job to do, and at some point the work has to get done. But I also know that you like to be a superstar, racing around, showing how fast you can complete the course. You have to realize that when you're recovering from burnout, you can't be on the Danica Patrick racetrack. You have to slow down a notch until you can safely get back up to that speed.

If you find yourself in a position where you have no choice but to take work home, you should reassess your work situation. Opting out, which is discussed later in this chapter, may be something you need to consider.

REINFORCE THE EFFORT, NOT THE OUTCOME

If you worked hard but didn't win the case, didn't get the new client, didn't make the sale, or didn't get the praise you think you deserve, reinforce yourself for your effort. No one is perfect (see chapter 5, if you have any doubts), and if you only reinforce the outcome, you're missing the point (and missing a lot of opportunities for reinforcement). The rewards can be the same ones we discussed previously—positive self-talk, going out to your favorite restaurant for an exquisite meal, buying something for yourself, mentally "staying in the moment," or whatever floats your boat (unless it's negative behavior, like drinking in excess or eating a gallon of ice cream).

CONSIDER A SUPPORT GROUP

Remember the chat we had about the benefits of chatting? Even if communicating your feelings with others isn't your strongest suit, sharing does help, if you give it a chance. A support group doesn't have to be a therapeutic group (although it could be); it can be a professional organization that provides support or mentoring, or it can be a casual group of friends getting together to vent or share ideas. Not only should this kind of group involvement help—because sharing your feelings with others often reduces stress—it should also reduce isolation.

SOCIALIZE OUTSIDE OF YOUR PROFESSIONAL GROUP

Always being around the same people in the same profession often just keeps you mired down in the stressors that are a part of your job. Make an effort to socialize with people outside your profession. This can provide fresh perspectives, stimulate new ideas, and help you discover previously untapped resources.

CONTROL YOUR DEVICES

Chapter 4 is devoted to how to take back control from your electronic devices. Read it again when you get weak-kneed and start to feel those devious creatures pulling you back into the virtual abyss. A major component of burnout is constant availability, and the biggest culprit is technology.

If you have a single e-mail account for work and personal contacts, consider setting up two separate accounts. Give your work contacts the work address and your personal contacts the personal address, and don't mix the two. And when you're off work, don't check your work account. The same applies for social networking sites, where many people mix business and personal contacts. Although it's harder to divide social networking sites into all business or all personal, you should do your best to keep your online "work talk" at work.

GIVE YOURSELF A BREAK

Take a break during your workday, even if it's just ten or fifteen minutes to walk around or get some fresh air. Find after-hours activities and interests unrelated to work to express your creativity. Reconnect with family and friends. Visit places you've never been before. You work hard. You deserve a break!

GET HELP WHEN NECESSARY

If you've been able to come this far, you've come a long way. But if you're still struggling after incorporating these changes into your life, it's time to get some professional advice. Signs that you should seek professional counseling include continuing, serious physical illness; debilitating anxiety or depression; thoughts of suicide or homicide; excessive use of alcohol or drugs; or an inability to competently and ethically practice your profession. Sometimes only a few sessions with a qualified therapist can go a long way in helping.

Some companies and certain professions, such as the legal profession, have employee assistance programs.[1] These programs offer assistance to employees or professionals struggling with emotional, stress-related, and/or substance abuse problems. If you're concerned that someone in the company will know you're seeking help, consider private therapy. It's confidential, and no one needs to know unless you want them to.

OPTING OUT

Opting out is a term that has been used to describe women who leave their careers, often because of difficulties they're having with balancing their career and child rearing. But opting out has also been used to describe women who leave for other reasons, such as stress and burnout.

The decision to opt out certainly can weigh heavily on the soul—and not just for financial reasons. Many high-achieving women pour a lot of blood, sweat, and tears into their careers. So, despite the stress their career may be causing them, they still often have a strong emotional connection to it.

But in cases of burnout, the bigger consideration has to be quality of life. I'll use the analogy of battered women here because it's actually not very far off from the dynamics of high-achieving women who stay in bad relationships with their jobs. In the case of battered women, it's actually quite rare to find women who hate their abusers. They don't like the abuse, but they often "love" the abuser and they hope he (or she, in some cases) is going to change. In fact, two of the biggest pulls that keep battered women in abusive relationships with their batterers are the emotional connection and the hope of change.

But, as it turns out, these women don't love the person who is beating them up day in and day out. They love the illusion of that person, the person they first met and fell in love with before the battering started, the person they still sometimes see glimpses of in between the beatings. And they hope that person—that illusion—will return. But despite promises of change from the abuser, the abuse usually continues.

In much the same way, burned-out, high-achieving women sometimes remain on the job, despite the fact that it may be beating them up day in and day out, because they love the illusion of the job based on a distant memory of what it once was and what it once meant to them. And they hope things will change.

But love or no love, illusion or not, when the circumstances don't change, the battered woman needs to get out of the relationship for two main reasons: (1) so she won't continue to be harmed or, worse, die at the hands of the batterer, and (2) so she can have a chance to live a happy, healthy, and fulfilled life.

The same holds true for burned-out women. Your job has beaten you up for years. If it doesn't change, especially after you call attention to the problems, it's not likely to change.

The other factor when you're considering opting out needs to be sustainability. I fully recognize that there are some women who don't have a choice in the matter. For financial reasons, they have to work, so opting out isn't an option. But opting out isn't restricted to leaving and not working at all. There's no reason it can't mean leaving and finding another place to work or even a different career. And that's where considerations of sustainability need to enter the picture.

As noted in chapter 7, burned-out bodies stop working at some point—physically, psychologically, or both. So if you have to work for financial reasons, what will you do *when*, *not if*, your body decides to take matters into its own hands and opts out for you? Wouldn't it be better to pursue a new career or new job that will present fresh and exciting challenges once your engine is reignited—one where you'll survive? Which is better: having one or two more years (or fewer) of burnout and distress before your body quits, or moving now (or as soon as you can find a new opportunity), probably to a lower-paying position but to a place where you have a chance to rediscover the challenges and excitement of a new opportunity to thrive and shine?

As I've said before, leaving a job, especially during trying economic times, is not a decision that should be made lightly. However, if you're burned out, it is an option that you should at least consider, given the serious physical and emotional consequences of staying in a situation that is unchanging and unhealthy.

DISCOVERING (OR REDISCOVERING) YOUR PASSION

Without exception, every high-achieving woman I've known in the past twenty-five years, as unique as they all have been, have had one thing in common—passion. They find something they love and they embrace it with all the energy and enthusiasm they can muster. They push themselves to climb higher and higher, to do better and better, and to achieve more and more because they're passionate about what they do.

But in many cases, the unyielding challenges they face on their journeys cause them to eventually run out of gas. That's what burnout does to high-achieving women—it extinguishes their passion, leaving them feeling physically exhausted and emotionally depleted.

In order to get back on the right track, refueled and ready to go, you have to find ways to resurrect that passion inside you. This may mean that you have to redefine your role at work, in your family, in your social network, or in all these areas. It may mean that you have to add things to your plate and take other things off, or at least find a way to redistribute the load. It may mean that you have to find a new passion that will offer more balance, so you can once again enjoy your life the way you once did. These are all answers that you need to discover for yourself, but you now have the road map that you need to help you find those answers.

OVERCOMING RESISTANCE

As you plot a new course and begin to make changes in your life, you should expect resistance, because other people—your colleagues, your family, and maybe even your friends—have likely come to depend on you doing it all and doing it well. As a result, there will likely be pulls from every direction, including from inside you, to keep things as they were, because the truth is that when things went well, they went very, very well. And despite your stress, you've probably done everything within your power to keep things as close to the status quo as possible, so it's very likely that those who are close to you, both at work and at home, may not even be aware of how distressed you are. But when you're burned out, maintaining the status quo is neither practical nor is it even possible, because at some point you're going to collapse.

Another reason for the resistance is fear. People are afraid of change for many reasons, but the one theme underlying all the reasons is fear of the risks involved. To change means to risk many things, such as the possible loss of your identity, the possible loss of your status, and the potential loss of a lifestyle to which you and others in your life have grown accustomed.

The best way to overcome this resistance is a two-step process: (1) commit to making the changes you need to make to restore your happiness, and (2) act as consistently as possible when you experience resistance. This may sound simple, but it's often quite difficult. To help you as you make your way through this process, it's important that you understand the typical phases people go through when they're faced with change.

There are many models that describe transition and change; however, the one I've found to be most applicable to the changes you'll be experiencing as you recover from burnout is a four-step model used by Flora/Elkind Associates to describe the process of organizational change.[2] I've adapted it slightly to what your personal experiences with change are likely to be.

The first phase of change is *denial*. By now, you should be past the denial stage, but you shouldn't necessarily expect the same from other people in your life. During this phase, you're likely to find that your coworkers, family, and friends seem to be going about their lives as if nothing has changed or is changing. Because they're in denial, they'll likely interact with you and have the same expectations of you that they've always had.

However, as you remain steadfast in your commitment to change, the people in your life will get to the point where they can no longer maintain their denial, which ushers in the second phase: *resistance*. This is the period in which others will likely make efforts, both actively and passively, to reverse the changes they are seeing in you and to try to get everything to return to what had been the status quo.

The resistance phase is likely to be your most difficult challenge, because a part of you will probably want to return to what you know, even though what you know is a burned-out shell of what you once were. You'll likely be afraid of what you don't know. You'll likely ask yourself a slew of questions: What will my life be like with all these changes? Will I be happy? Will my lifestyle change? Will I fail? All these questions are normal, but you should trust in yourself and the plan you've developed. You should trust that what you're doing will have both short-term and long-term benefits, because the alternative is to return to a life of exhaustion, unhappiness, and a sense of hopelessness. And you should trust yourself enough to know that, if at any point your plans need to be adjusted, you're capable of doing that as well. This is your life and your plan. Nothing is written in stone.

Once you move through resistance, the third phase of change is *exploration*. This is when you can expect to feel in yourself and see in others more positive feelings toward the changes you have made and continue to make. By now, you and everyone else in your life realize that the world isn't coming to an end. It's different than what it once was, but if all has gone as planned, it should be different in a good way. As a result, the fears should be fading, and your sense of joy and satisfaction should be rising.

The final phase is *commitment*. The road up to now probably hasn't been an easy one, but you've done it! You've committed to a new way of living your life, and you should now see support from others for the changes you've made in your life. You should be feeling a sense of renewed passion, energy, and excitement about the present and the future. You're back to your high-achieving self. But the lessons from the past should not be forgotten.

ACHIEVEMENT IS IMPORTANT, BUT . . .

When I was in the process of writing this book, a close friend of mine shared a story with me. Written anonymously, it should serve as a powerful reminder that the corner office is not everything.

> *First, I was dying to finish high school and start college.*
> *And then I was dying to finish college and start working.*
> *Then I was dying to marry and have children.*
> *And then I was dying for my children to grow old enough so I*
>   *could go back to work.*
> *And then I was dying to retire.*

And now I'm dying . . .
and suddenly I realized I forgot to live.[3]

Achievement and success are important, but they're not worth sacrificing everything for. "Having it all" is a myth, an unachievable goal. But that doesn't make what you've accomplished and what you will accomplish in the future any less amazing, nor does it make you and who you are any less extraordinary. You are a unique woman, which is why I encourage you to take every opportunity to set the course that *you* want to travel, so that at the end of what will be an amazing race, you'll be proud of how you ran it.

EPILOGUE

The focus of this book has been on approaches that you, as an individual, can take to combat stress in your life and reduce your risk for burnout. However, decades of research have made it clear that burnout is *not* an individual problem—it's an organizational problem, fueled by dysfunction in the structure and functioning of the workplace itself.[1]

As Christina Maslach and Michael Leiter write in their book *The Truth about Burnout*, "We agree that people experience burnout as a personal problem and that they have a part to play in preventing or alleviating it, but we do not agree that people are totally responsible for its occurrence or its solution."[2] In fact, they go on to say that "[w]hen an organizational environment is unresponsive to people—to their aspirations, their limitations, and the way they work—chronic burnout is the inevitable result."[3] Therefore, if reducing burnout is the goal, companies *must* be part of the solution.

Unfortunately, many companies today continue to ignore the significant impact stress has on their employees and the role they themselves play in creating that stress. With a focus on the bottom line, they work their employees to the brink of burnout and beyond, offering little to no flexibility or assistance, and then blame the employees when they can no longer keep up the pace.

Short-sighted? Absolutely. The toll of human stress costs businesses billions of dollars each year in sick leave, workers' compensation, absenteeism, health insurance, and lost productivity.[4] But these aren't the only costs.

The loss of talent is a cost that is hard to put a price tag on. The levels at which high-achieving women work make them a difficult asset to easily replace. Next, there are the costs associated with finding a suitable replacement. Recruitment costs for top-level employees can be steep. There are headhunter fees and advertising costs. There is lost time spent on going over résumés and conducting interviews of potential replacements. And once a replacement is found, indirect costs mount up in the form of clients who may leave the company when the employee leaves, lowered productivity because the replacement lacks experience, and the time it takes to train new employees, no matter how experienced they may be.[5] Still, despite all these costs, the problem of stress in the workplace is unfortunately ignored more often than not.

Why does this happen, especially at a time in history when businesses have become so cost-conscious? Maslach and Leiter explain, "Despite its value, an organizational approach to burnout is more complex and therefore more challenging. Because people tend to think of events as being caused by individuals rather than by groups or social processes, it's not easy to conceive of an intervention in organizational terms."[6] The authors further note that because change often disrupts the normal procedures and power structure of a company, any attempts to intervene at an organizational level tend to be met with strong resistance.

That's not to say that all companies turn a blind eye to the problem. Some companies recognize the consequences of employee burnout. Still, it's often the case that their narrow understanding of the problem leads them to view burnout as purely an individual issue rather than a work-induced problem, which can make the problem even worse.

Although there are some individual factors that can increase stress in the lives of high-achieving women, individual solutions alone are inadequate to address the breadth and depth of the problem. As a systemic problem, caused largely by structural and functional troubles in the workplace, burnout requires an intelligent, well-conceived, well-developed, broad-based, and future-focused organizational plan to most effectively address it.[7] Unfortunately, a company's only "plan" often is to have employees attend prepackaged stress-management workshops, which can lead to their own problems.

First, stress-management workshops, by their focus on individual strategies to manage stress, intimate that stress is the workers' responsibility. This kind of message can set up burnout victims for failure, especially high-achieving women because they tend to be problem solvers by nature. When faced with a problem, they try to fix it. Yet, when they attempt to fix the stressors in their workplaces, they often find themselves stranded, alone on an island, with their companies staying far away from the shoreline, unwilling to take ownership of their share of the problem.

Second, stress-management programs typically focus on general approaches for *individuals*, such as breathing exercises, relaxation exercises, meditation, and guided imagery. Not only do these generic approaches not take into consideration the unique needs of each person in the workshop, but the techniques they teach, though they may be helpful when part of a tailored, comprehensive program, can go only so far under these circumstances.

Let's say, for example, that you decide to follow the advice you were given in a stress-management workshop, and you select yoga classes to reduce stress. You do your breathing exercises while you're driving to your early morning yoga class. You take the class and come out of it feeling pretty good. You jump in your car and head off to work. But on the drive, your phone rings. It's your son. He forgot his homework on the table and he's going to get an F if you don't drive home, get it, and bring it to him before his next class. You call your husband, but he's in a meeting and can't help. You race home, grab the homework, rush over to the school, and drop it off just in time. But now you're late for an important meeting at work where you're supposed to be presenting a proposal. You call your boss to explain what happened, and he responds, "If you can't handle the heat, maybe you should go back to the kitchen" (or some other equally offensive sexist remark). And you haven't even arrived at work yet!

Your hour of yoga—your individual approach to stress relief—has been effectively destroyed by technological, family, and workplace stressors that place you in a no-win situation. A rare occurrence? Not in the lives of many high-achieving women who often feel pulled in a hundred different directions, and not just by the things *they* do to themselves. It's the totality of their life circumstances. My point is that a one-size-fits-all approach to stress management often doesn't help high-achieving women very much.

Finally, burnout is an extraordinarily complex problem that often takes years to develop. Therefore, it's incredibly naive, bordering on absurd, to believe that sending burnout victims to a workshop, regardless of its length, will effect the type of change that would be necessary to make even a dent in the problem. It's analogous to putting a Band-Aid on a gaping wound. All too often, the worker bleeds out before the company even realizes it.

I'm not implying that companies are *trying* to kill their workers (although some burned-out employees may feel that way), nor am I trying to deter companies that want to help. However, they have to make sure that their attempt to "cure the disease" doesn't "kill the patient." In some cases, as Dr. Steven Berglas points out in *Reclaiming the Fire*, generic stress-management programs for employees may actually make their symptoms worse.[8]

"The problems caused by prepackaged therapeutic or morale-building programs are significant and extensive," says Dr. Berglas. "People who participate in these programs and fail to experience symptomatic relief may suffer a worsening of the problems they sought to remedy."[9] The phenomenon he is referring to is called a *negative placebo effect*.

Most people are familiar with the term *placebo* in a neutral or positive sense. The placebo effect occurs when a patient is given some kind of treatment, often in the form of a pill, that has no therapeutic or pharmacologic agent that would make it effective, yet the patient *believes* that it does. If, after receiving the "treatment," the patient's symptoms lessen or disappear, the placebo is credited with causing the "effect." Thus, it's called the *placebo effect*.

But what happens in situations when the treatment—in this case, stress-management training—is supposed to relieve symptoms but then doesn't? In this scenario, burned-out employees may experience a negative placebo effect. The employee attends the training, expecting it to reduce her stress. But if relief doesn't come, which isn't uncommon in cases of burnout, she may think there is something wrong with her or that her symptoms are much worse than she first thought, which can lead to an increase in sadness, hopelessness, and frustration. In short, what was supposed to relieve stress may end up actually creating more stress.[10]

Am I saying that stress-management workshops never help? No, they help some people. But in cases of burnout, if there is relief, it is often short-lived. And even if the stress relief helps, it doesn't address the systemic problems that create stress in the workplace. The reality is that to move into the future and meet the needs of women and families in today's workforce, companies need to do their part

Fortunately, some are. In fact, for a few companies on the cutting edge, the future looks very good for employees who are seeking more balance in their lives, more opportunities for creativity on the job, and less stress in their work environment.[11]

INNOVATIVE WORKPLACE APPROACHES TO BURNOUT

Flexibility

Flexibility in the workplace has become such a central issue for today's families that the White House is even getting involved. On March 23, 2010, the office of the press secretary released a statement announcing that President Obama plans to host a "Forum on Workplace Flexibility" at the White

House. In the statement, the president is quoted as saying, "Millions of women and men across the country struggle to balance the demands of their jobs and the needs of their families. Too often, caring for a child or an aging parent can strain a career—sometimes to the point of job loss."[12] The president goes on to say that as the parents of two young children, he and First Lady Michelle Obama understand the challenges facing America's working families and are looking forward to hearing ideas at the forum that will help to create flexible work environments so that working parents don't have to choose between their careers and their families.

Most employees seem to concur with the president's sentiments. Surveys consistently show that one of the most highly ranked perks workers want from their companies is flexibility in their work schedules.[13] This is particularly true for working women.

One of the biggest success stories for flexibility in the workplace is BT, a telecommunications company in the United Kingdom. Its innovative approaches not only reduce stress in workers' lives and help the company retain workers, they also substantially increase the company's profits. At BT, employees have the option of requesting flexible work schedules, which can include part-time, flex-time, home working, a compressed workweek, job sharing, annualized hours, and term-time working (a work schedule that allows parents to take off when their children are off from school). BT promotes this kind of flexibility by giving all employees access to sites that allow them to work online anywhere in real time. And from the look of things, their innovative approach has been amazingly successful.

Of BT's one hundred thousand employees, sixty thousand have flexible schedules. Ten percent of employees work from home, 5 percent work part-time, and several hundred share jobs. Their attrition rate is at 3 percent, and, after maternity leave, 99 percent of women return to work. This is in contrast to the UK average of only 47 percent of women who return to work after giving birth. BT conservatively estimates that their flex program saves the company over nine million dollars a year in recruitment and training costs. Absenteeism is also down to almost 3 percent, which is much lower than the UK average of 11 percent.[14]

Although it's far from being the norm, an increasing number of companies are beginning to offer flexible work schedules to employees. In the United States, companies such as Procter & Gamble, CISCO Systems, IBM, American Express, Citi, Ernst & Young, and Deloitte boast flexible work arrangements as a core element of their companies.[15] In fact, of the top "100 Best Companies" chosen by *Working Mother* in 2009, all offer telecommuting and flexible schedules, 98 percent offer job-sharing opportunities, and 94 percent offer compressed workweeks.[16]

Not only do these programs benefit both the worker and the company immediately and directly, they also benefit the future of companies. Because flexible work schedules are in such high demand, companies that offer such perks should be able to pick the cream of the crop from applicants vying for positions. Flexibility also increases productivity, makes workers feel as if they have some control over what happens to them in the workplace, and improves the overall mood of the workplace, which is likely to significantly reduce stress levels of employees who are able to take advantage of flexible work programs.

However, the operative words here are employees *who are able* to take advantage of them. Flexible scheduling options aren't helpful if workers don't feel they will work to their advantage. In order for flexible work arrangements to be effective, a company needs to have full support of the program at all levels of management. If management frowns upon workers who ask for flex schedules or if there is a stigma associated with using them, they will be of little value to employees. In fact, having flexibility available "on paper" but not in practice is only likely to add to a worker's frustration, disillusionment with the company, and overall stress, which is what happened to Shana, an executive at a moderately sized accounting firm.

Shana had requested a flex schedule for three months, so that she could help her mother recover from surgery. Her request was approved, but Shana said she would "never do it again." She explained, "The whole time I was working from home, I felt like my boss resented it. The way he spoke to me, the way he looked at me when I'd go into the office to pick up something. It was like he was grudgingly doing me a favor. I went back early because it wasn't worth the pressure I was feeling. If they don't want a flex program, then they shouldn't advertise it as a perk." Shana's experience offers a good example of how a flexible program that is not supported by management can be as stressful to employees as not having a program at all.

Comprehensive Benefits Programs

The North Carolina–based software firm SAS, with satellite offices in Massachusetts, won the honor of being named *Fortune* magazine's "Best Company to Work For" in 2010.[17] Offering unlimited sick leave, 90 percent insurance premium coverage, a free gym, a medical center for employees, high-quality childcare, and a summer camp for children, SAS tries to keep its employees happy, motivated, and loyal—and it seems to be working. The company boasts an annual employee turnover rate of only 2 percent, and the average worker has been with the company over ten years.[18]

Abbott Laboratories is another company that offers its employees an impressive benefits program. The program, which is called Work-Life Benefits, offers flexible start/stop times, job sharing, telecommuting, compressed workweeks, and reduced workweeks. Abbott says its program is rooted in three global demographic trends: the aging of the workforce, the increasingly critical role of women in the workforce, and the changing work attitudes of younger employees seeking job opportunities that offer more balance between work and family. In keeping with this philosophy, Abbott also offers employees on-site childcare, emergency childcare assistance, on-site parenting and counseling services, kindergarten programs, and holiday childcare. The company also offers a "Mothers at Work" program, which helps new mothers manage their breastfeeding schedule at work and provides twenty-four-hour access to lactation consultants.[19]

Stage-of-Life Flexibility

Some companies have incorporated flexibility into the workplace by offering it at various stages of life when employees are most likely to need it. In these companies, not all employees qualify for flexible work schedules, but when workers are going through a stage of life where more flexibility is needed, they can apply for it. These stages may include maternity leave and early childcare times, paternity leave, a return to school, and elderly care responsibilities. Once the stage-of-life issue has resolved, the employees are welcomed back to their regular position. This type of program is designed to offer employees flexibility at times in their lives when they most need it. But again, for this to work, top management needs to support its use.

Sabbaticals

For those workers who find themselves in situations that require a more extended break from work, some companies are now offering sabbatical programs. For example, Deloitte, an international accounting and consulting firm, offers the option of a sabbatical to employees who want to pursue not only professional goals but personal ones as well. Recently, one of Deloitte's managers took a three-month sabbatical to train for a climb up Mount Everest.[20]

Opportunities for Creativity

Smart companies realize that big brains need time to think creatively outside the box. They realize that these kinds of opportunities reenergize employees and help them see things in new and innovative ways. Google seems to understand this very well; in fact, it created a schedule around it. Conceived by Google cofounder, Sergey Brin, engineers and managers at Google split their work schedule 70/20/10. Seventy percent of their work time is dedicated to core product development; 20 percent is devoted to new, but related projects and business; and the remaining 10 percent is considered "white space"—time when employees can work on anything they want that could possibly generate new ideas or business.[21] Companies that use this approach are likely to find that giving employees time to engage their brains in creative ways reduces stress and makes for more motivated and less burned-out employees who generate creative ideas, which benefits both the employee and the company.

Supporting Wellness

Another way to reduce stress in the workplace is to emphasize wellness by making it a part of the workday. Some companies are adding gyms to their work spaces and encouraging workers to take advantage of them before, during, or after hours. Other companies support wellness by emphasizing the importance of taking time off and encouraging employees to take advantage of maternity leave. Through the promotion of health and wellness, companies are likely to find employees taking fewer sick days and having better attitudes at work.

Eliminating Redundancy

In every company, unnecessary and redundant policies and procedures abound. The only reason they remain is because they've been around for so long that everyone just routinely follows them. Recognizing that redundancy is a waste of resources, some companies have decided to take a closer look at their policies and procedures to determine which ones can be eliminated without affecting the normal flow of business or the bottom line. In doing so, some companies discovered that policies that required weekly meetings could just as easily be handled through an office memo or e-mail. Others discovered forms and paperwork that were redundant, time consuming, and unnecessary. By eliminating redundancies and unnecessary policies and procedures, companies not only increase the amount of time workers have to handle important and relevant work but also reduce workers' stress levels by taking away mundane and frustrating tasks that serve no purpose.

Increase Workers' Participation in Decision Making

One of the most stressful aspects of work is when employees feel as if they have no control over what happens to them in the company. To reduce that stress, some companies have moved toward a more participatory model in which, whenever possible, workers are allowed to discuss aspects of their jobs that make their lives more difficult. This helps to give employees a sense of power and control, the feeling that they can play an active role in removing obstacles that they see as getting in the way of their overall productivity and performance, thereby reducing frustration and stress.

Increase Positive Feedback about Performance

Most of the time, workers hear feedback only when they make a mistake or when something goes wrong. In psychology (and elsewhere), this is known as punishment. The intent of punishment is to reduce negative behavior. However, punishment does nothing to strengthen positive behavior.

The best way to get more out an employee is to strengthen positive behavior, not punish negative behavior. This happens when employers use reinforcement. Reinforcement can take many forms. It can range from a smile or a pat on the back to a big raise or bonus. It can come in the form of verbal praise or a printed certificate. It can also come from letting employees know when they did something right or did something exceptionally well.

The problem for many high-achieving women is that their work is almost always exceptional. When excellence happens so frequently, it's easy for employers to fall into the trap of simply expecting it, which reduces the likelihood that the work will be reinforced. Employers can avoid this trap by training themselves, through notes and reminders, to say something positive at least once a day to employees. By doing this, employees are more likely to feel appreciated and possibly less stressed.

Increase Opportunities for Social Support

Some companies try to reduce worker's stress by providing them with opportunities to meet with coworkers and bosses and share their experiences—both positive and negative. This not only gives workers the opportunity to vent, it also gives them the opportunity to see that they're not alone. They get to see that coworkers are experiencing the same kinds of problems and feeling the same kinds of stress. They are also able to share strategies for what works for them in resolving problems and reducing stress.

Increase Opportunities to Offer Feedback

Research coming out of the United Kingdom has found that companies that give employees opportunities to provide feedback to their bosses on their management skills can reduce workplace stress. When handled properly and sensitively, managers who receive feedback are more likely to change their management style and to show positive management behavior that prevents and reduces stress in their team.[22] Employees are also likely to benefit because it gives them an opportunity to express their opinions and feel as if they have some control over what happens in the workplace.

Forewarned Is Forearmed: Burnout Prevention Programs

Some workplaces tackle burnout in a more direct way by offering training programs designed to help employees anticipate burnout and prevent it. The model for this type of anticipatory training program was developed by Marlene Kramer after she observed a great deal of burnout in the nursing profession.[23] Although originally developed for nurses, the concept can be applied to almost any field.

The goal of the program is to reduce the shock many workers experience when they suddenly realize that their dream job and their actual job are not one in the same. Many workers go into a new job with idealistic expectations and preset notions. But once they begin, they start getting hit by doses of reality. The differences between what they expected and what they are getting create stress, which can eventually lead to burnout.

Kramer's approach is to purposefully challenge these ideals, but in a way that encourages workers to learn and to use constructive strategies for coping with the realities of the job. The first phase involves producing a mild form of reality by showing new workers the kinds of unexpected things they may encounter on the job. This is often provided in the form of real-life examples that have happened on the job or that were experienced by actual workers who come in and tell their stories.

The second phase gives workers a taste of the negative and tedious aspects of the job that they may not have anticipated. This is done by exposing new workers to mundane (yet required) paperwork, unpopular policies that have to be followed, and cumbersome procedures that must be adhered to. The purpose is to let workers know that not all aspects of the job are exciting, that there are times when the work will be boring, unfulfilling, and frustrating.

Phase three introduces workers to supervisors and coworkers whose job is to give new workers a realistic understanding of what will be expected of them on the job. And the final phase teaches workers principles of conflict resolution and negotiation in the hope that they will use them to effectively manage conflict when it arises in the future. Teaching workers how to effect change in their workplace when they come up against something they don't like or don't feel comfortable with gives them a sense of control over what is happening to them, which often reduces stress and lessens the likelihood of burnout.

The strength of this type of training is that it's aimed at prevention. It serves as a reality check, allowing workers to anticipate the obstacles that lie ahead. Because it's educational in nature, it works well with new or beginning employees. For the same reason, it isn't particularly effective for workers who are already burned out.

WHY COMPANIES SHOULD SUPPORT CHANGE

Because, as previously noted, women assume the majority of childcare, extended family care, and household responsibilities, the changes I've been describing are certainly a benefit to women in particular. However, women clearly are not the sole beneficiaries of positive changes in the workplace. Companies that incorporate flexibility, emphasize wellness, and promote stress reduction in their work philosophies and workplaces benefit greatly, as does society as a whole—and not just because it's a nice thing to do.

Despite their struggles to combat stress, women have become a powerful force behind economic growth. They represent the fastest-growing segment of small-business owners. They control large amounts of money. They invest. They make the majority of the purchasing decisions for their families[24]—and they're not just spending it on shoes and clothes, as stereotypes suggest. According to Marti Barletta, author of *Marketing to Women: How to Understand, Reach, and Increase Your Share of the World's Largest Market Segment*, "These days women are buying cars, computers, and carpeting, and shelling out the cash for insurance policies, investments, and improvements to the home as well."[25]

So, from a business perspective, it just makes sense to support workplace programs that support working women, not only because they're bright, talented, and hardworking but also because it's smart business. If women are making the large majority of the spending decisions, why wouldn't companies want them in top positions so that the company can better understand the wants and needs of such a huge customer base?

High-achieving women aren't just bodies taking up a chair in the company. Their presence makes a real difference. In fact, several studies have found that companies in which women are well represented on executive boards perform better financially than those with little or no female presence—a lot better, in fact. According to Catalyst, companies with the highest number of female board members had a 53 percent larger return on equity, a 42 percent larger return on sales, and a whopping 66 percent higher return on invested capital. These findings were stable across most companies, regardless of their focus and product.[26]

Studies in the European market show the same kinds of results. The consulting firm McKinsey and Company found that the stock value of European companies with the highest proportion of women in power climbed by 64 percent over a two-year period. The firm also discovered that compared to companies with no senior-level women, companies with three or more women in upper management received higher ratings in leadership, direction, accountability, motivation, and many other dimensions related to strong organization.[27]

As writer Rebecca Tuhus-Dubrow of the *Boston Globe* sees it, "The mounting body of evidence represents an important twist in the debate over women in business. For decades, women's advancement has been seen as an issue of fairness and equality. Now some researchers are saying it should also be seen in another way: as a smart way to make money."[28]

But the benefits of female leaders in the workplace aren't just financial. When women are involved in leadership positions, new ideas are generated and changes start to be made. For example, as politicians, females are more likely to tackle and advocate for important social and family services, such as women's access to childcare and healthcare, child support enforcement, and education. They are also more likely to raise awareness of troubling social issues, such as child abuse, violence against women, and school violence, and are often vigorous advocates for legislation to address these problems.[29]

The bottom line is that when women are involved, changes happen—good changes. However, just opening the door and letting women in will do nothing (but add to their stress levels) without change from inside the company—change led by innovative approaches like the ones I've described to reduce the stressors that ultimately wear down high-achieving women and burn them out. Companies that can accomplish this—that will open the door to upper-level positions for women and will create innovative workplace solutions to help them better deal with the multiple levels of stress in their lives—will be our future's most successful and richly diverse workplaces.[30]

WHAT DOES THE FUTURE HOLD?

Companies are changing, but not quickly enough. For those who are fortunate enough to work for companies that understand the needs of working women and their families, the future looks bright. But there are many more companies that simply ignore these needs, leaving far too many women feeling stressed out and burned out. And for the new generation of workers—

the "children of the gender revolution," as Kathleen Gerson calls them—the uncertainty of what the workplace can offer them with respect to balancing their career needs, personal needs, and family needs is frightening indeed.[31]

In *The Unfinished Revolution*, Gerson describes a generation of up-and-coming high achievers with big dreams and high hopes for a bright career, an egalitarian partnership, and a happy family. Yet, "amid time-demanding workplaces, pressures to parent intensively, and rising standards for a ful-filling relationship, they harbor considerable doubts about the chances of achieving their ideals."[32] Women of this new working generation don't see themselves as having to be dependent on men, nor do they want to be. They see a career as an essential way to ensure their independence and to provide themselves with the security they need to support themselves and their children. They want a family, but one that isn't defined by rigid gender roles. And they're looking for workplaces that can provide balance so they can enjoy the benefits of both a successful career and a strongly connected family.

And so, as they say, the writing is on the wall. Older women, younger women, and all those in between are looking for change. They're tired of being pulled in so many different directions. They want more balanced lives and they realize that's not attainable under the business models of most workplaces today. They want flexible schedules, they want options, and they desperately want less stress in their lives.

Knowing this, and knowing where future generations seem to be heading, companies today have amazing opportunities for enormous growth and success. The more options companies offer to their workers, the more successful they are likely to be in attracting the best, the brightest, and the most talented women in the world. The more successful they are in getting these talented women, the more successful companies will be. And the more flexibility these women have in their lives, the more successful and stress-free they will be. It's a future that's definitely coming. I only hope that it is sooner rather than later.

IN THE MEANTIME . . .

Until that time comes, it's incumbent upon you, as a high-achieving woman, to understand the magnitude, the seriousness, and the potential consequences of the stressors you're facing both inside and outside the workplace. As we've discussed, there is a lot of debris flying at you from all directions, and if you don't want it to knock you out of the race, then you need to protect yourself from it. You need an effective plan—a plan that will not only keep you in the race but also keep you moving along at the speeds you were born to travel. You now have the tools you need to develop that plan, to bring about healthy changes in your life that will keep your engine running as smoothly as possible for a long time.

You also have a unique opportunity. By calling attention to the inequity and the injustice—the double standards, double binds, and stereotypes—in the workplace and elsewhere, not only can you change your own path, you can also make the road less bumpy for those coming up behind you. In the words of Amelia Earhart, "Some of us have great runways already built for us. If you have one, take off. But if you don't have one, realize it's your responsibility to grab a shovel and build one for yourself and for those who will follow you."[33] It is only through your efforts that your runway will expand and ultimately pave the way to make the ride smoother for the amazingly talented and passionate women who will follow in your footsteps.

Each individual and each generation leaves behind a legacy. Let yours be a legacy of strength and resiliency that will serve as the foundation that builds the paths upon which future generations can soar.

NOTES

INTRODUCTION

1. Christina Maslach, Michael P. Leiter, and Wilmar Schaufeli, "Measuring Burnout," in *The Oxford Handbook of Organizational Well-Being*, ed. Susan Cartwright and Cary L. Cooper (New York: Oxford University Press, 2009), pp. 88–89.

2. Ibid., p. 90.

3. Debra Cassens Weiss, "Firm Hit over Partner's Hiring Question: How Can We Identify New Mom's Commitment?" *ABA Journal*, February 16, 2010, accessed February 16, 2010, http://www.abajournal.com/news/article/firm_hit_over_partners _hiring_question_how_can_we_identify_new_moms_commitm.

4. Lois Joy, et al., "The Bottom Line: Corporate Performance and Women's Representation on Boards," Catalyst, October 2007, accessed March 25, 2010, http://www.catalyst.org/publication/200/the-bottom-line-corporate-performance -and-womens-representation-on-boards; Michele L. Swers, *The Difference Women Make: The Policy Impact of Women in Congress* (Chicago: University of Chicago Press, 2002), pp. 126–28.

CHAPTER 1: The Amazing Race

1. Penny Coleman, *Rosie the Riveter, Women Working on the Home Front in World War II* (New York: Crown Publishers, 1995), pp. 97–101.

2. Betty Friedan, *The Feminine Mystique* (New York: W. W. Norton 1963).

3. Ann-Marie Imbornoni, "Women's Rights Movement in the U.S.: Timeline of Key Events in the Women's Rights Movement, 1848–1920," Infoplease, accessed February 20, 2010, http://www.infoplease.com/spot/womenstimeline1.html.

4. Catherine Rampell, "Women Now a Majority in American Workplaces," *New York Times*, February 5, 2010, accessed March 17, 2010, http://www.nytimes.com/ 2010/02/06/business/economy/06women.html.

5. *The Double-Bind Dilemma for Women in Leadership: Damned If You Do, Doomed If You Don't*, research report for Catalyst (New York: Catalyst, 2007), p. 3.

6. Maria Shriver, "The Unfinished Revolution," *Time*, October 26, 2009, p. 35.

7. Nancy Gibbs, "What Women Want Now," *Time*, October 26, 2009, p. 30.

8. Lauren Streib, "The Year's Top-Earning Musicians," Forbes.com, June 22,

2009, accessed March 26, 2010, http://www.forbes.com/2009/06/22/top-earning -musicians-business-entertainment-musicians.html.

9. "Sandra Bullock Rakes It In: Actress Beats Johnny Depp to Be Crowned Highest Earning in Hollywood," News of the World, March 1, 2009, accessed March 26, 2010, http://www.newsoftheworld.co.uk/showbiz/659440/Actress-beats-Depp -to -be-crowned-highest-earning-in-Hollywood.html.

10. Joe Neumaier, "Oscars 2010: Kathryn Bigelow's 'Hurt Locker' Wins Best Director," NYDailyNews.com, March 7, 2010, accessed March 26, 2010, http://www .nydailynews.com/entertainment/movies/2010/03/07/2010-03-07_he_waltzes_to _early _oscar _win_austrian_actor_nailed_oily_nazi_in_basterds.html.

11. Andrea Ford and Dierdre Van Dyk, "Then & Now: A Statistical Look Back from the 1970s to Today," Time, October 26, 2009, p. 27.

12. US Department of Labor, Women in the Labor Force: A Databook (Washington, DC: Bureau of Labor Statistics, September 2009), pp. 53–54.

13. Herminia Ibarra and Morton T. Hansen, "Women CEOs: Why So Few?" Harvard Business Review, December 21, 2009, accessed February 2, 2010, http://blogs.hbr.org/cs/2009/12/women_ceo_why_so_few.html.

14. Emily Barker, "Stuck in the Middle," AmericanLawyer.com, June 1, 2009, accessed March 19, 2010, http://www.law.com/jsp/tal/PubArticleTAL.jsp?id =1202430856584; Hilary Russ, "Women Still Number Too Few in Partner Ranks," Law360, December 11, 2009, accessed March 19, 2010, http://www.law360.com/ articles/135591.

15. "Women, Minorities, and Persons with Disabilities in Science and Engineering," National Science Foundation, December 2008, accessed March 19, 2010, http://www.nsf.gov/statistics/wmpd/figh-1.htm.

16. "Women in Elective Office 2010," Center for American Women and Politics, Rutgers University, Eagleton Institute of Politics, March 3, 2010, accessed March 18, 2010, http://www.cawp.rutgers.edu/fast_facts/index.php.

17. "Gender Differences in Voter Turnout," Center for American Women and Politics, Rutgers University, Eagleton Institute of Politics, November 2009, accessed March 18, 2010, http://www.cawp.rutgers.edu/fast_facts/voters/turnout.php.

18. Richard Fry and D'Vera Cohn, "New Economics of Marriage: The Rise of Wives," PewResearchCenterPublications, January 19, 2010, accessed March 18, 2010, http://pewresearch.org/pubs/1466/economics-marriage-rise-of-wives.

19. Gibbs, "What Women Want Now," p. 26.

20. Betsy Stevenson and Justin Wolfers, "The Paradox of Declining Female Happiness," American Economic Journal: Economic Policy 1, no. 2 (2009): 190.

21. "APA Poll Finds Women Bear Brunt of Nation's Stress, Financial Downturn," American Psychological Association, October 7, 2008, accessed February 21, 2010, http://www.apa.org/news/press/releases/2008/10/stress-women.aspx.

22. Sylvia Ann Hewlett et al., *Sustaining High Performance in Difficult Times* (New York: Center for Work-Life Policy, 2008), p. 6.

CHAPTER 2: Road Conditions

1. "The Union Movement's Proud Past," AFL-CIO, accessed February 1, 2010, http://www.aflcio.org/aboutus/history/history/.

2. Sylvia Ann Hewlett et al., *Seduction and Risk: The Emergence of Extreme Jobs* (New York: Center for Work-Life Policy, 2007), p. 9.

3. NFI Research, "Work Time," accessed October 19, 2010, http://workyour strengths.net/powerpoint/2009/work_time_2009.pdf.

4. Hewlett, *Seduction and Risk*, p. 6.

5. Dee Dee Myers, *Why Women Should Rule the World* (New York: Harper-Collins Publishers, 2008), p. 26.

6. Hewlett, *Seduction and Risk*, p. 3.

7. Ibid., p. 4.

8. Ibid., pp. 4–5.

9. Ibid., p. 5.

10. Ibid., p. 6.

11. Ibid., p. 11.

12. Shelley E. Taylor et al., "Biobehavioral Responses to Stress in Females: Tend-and-Befriend, Not Fight-or-Flight," *Psychological Review* 107, no. 3 (2000): 411–29; Shelley Taylor, "Tend and Befriend: Biobehavioral Bases of Affiliation under Stress," *Current Directions in Psychological Science* 15, no. 6 (2006): 273–77.

13. John M. Gibbons, "I Can't Get No . . . Job Satisfaction, That Is," Conference Board, accessed February 25, 2010, January 2010, http://www.conference-board .org/publications/describe.cfm?id=1727.

14. Gregory Bateson et al., "Toward a Theory of Schizophrenia," *Behavioral Sciences* 1 (1956): 251–64.

15. Paul Gibney, "The Double Bind Theory: Still Crazy-Making after All These Years," *Psychotherapy in Australia* 12, no. 3 (2006): 50.

16. *The Double-Bind Dilemma for Women in Leadership: Damned If You Do, Doomed If You Don't*, research report for Catalyst (New York: Catalyst, 2007), p. 15.

17. *Women "Take Care," Men "Take Charge": Stereotyping of U.S. Business Leaders Exposed*, research report for Catalyst (New York: Catalyst, 2005), p. 6.

18. *Double-Bind Dilemma for Women in Leadership*, p. 1.

19. Ibid., p. 3.

20. *Women "Take Care," Men "Take Charge,"* p. 4.

21. *Double-Bind Dilemma for Women in Leadership*, p. 5.

22. Ibid., p. 11.

23. Pamela Stone, *Opting Out: Why Women Really Quit Careers and Head Home* (Berkley: University of California Press, 2007), p. 104.

24. *Women "Take Care," Men "Take Charge,"* p. 5.

25. Deborah Tannen, *Talking from 9 to 5* (New York: Harper, 1994).

26. Ibid., pp. 314–15.

27. Ibid., p. 13.

28. Although Tannen doesn't use the specific dichotomies I use in this book to describe communication styles, the information for this section was mostly developed from her work (although I opted not to include gender-specific commentary, as she does in *Talking from 9 to 5*). For readers interested in gender-specific references and more comprehensive coverage of communication styles in the workplace, please see Tannen's *Talking from 9 to 5*.

29. Tannen, *Talking from 9 to 5*, p. 23.

30. Ibid., pp. 58–59.

31. Ibid., p. 40.

32. Ibid., p. 59.

33. Ibid., p. 23.

34. Caroline Turner, "Hillary Clinton and the Double Bind: Hope for a More Balanced Kind of Leadership," Athena Group, 2008, p. 3, accessed February 18, 2010, http://www.athenagroup.biz/whitepapers/whitepapers.html; Arianna Huffington, "Sleep Challenge 2010: Getting Horizontal on the Way to Gender Parity," *Huffington Post*, February 1, 2010, accessed March 19, 2010, http://www.huffingtonpost.com/arianna-huffington/sleep-challenge-2010-gett_b_444782.html.

35. Tannen, *Talking from 9 to 5*, p. 136.

36. Ibid., p. 170.

37. Ibid., pp. 26–28, 61–63.

38. Ibid., pp. 34–35.

39. Ibid., pp. 153–55.

40. Joan C. Howden, "Competitive and Collaborative Communication Style: American Men and Women, American Men and Japanese Men," *International Communication Studies* 4, no. 1 (1994): 49–58; Deborah Tannen, "The Power of Talk: Who Gets Heard and Why," *Harvard Business Review* (September–October 1995): 140–41.

41. Tannen, "Power of Talk," p. 141.

42. Tannen, *Talking from 9 to 5*, pp. 78–106.

43. Ibid., p. 94.

44. Ibid., p. 88.

45. Linda Naranjo-Huebl, "From Peek-a-boo to Sarcasm: Women's Humor as a Means of Both Connection and Resistance," *Studies in Prolife Feminism* 1, no. 4 (1995): 343–72.

46. Mary Crawford, *Talking Difference: On Gender and Language* (London: Sage Publications, 1995), pp. 136–41; Nancy A. Walker and Zita Dresner, "Women's Humor in America," in *What's So Funny: Humor in American Culture*, ed. Nancy A. Walker (Wilmington, DE: Scholarly Resources, 1998), p. 173.

47. Tannen, *Talking from 9 to 5*, pp. 72–73.

48. Miranda Hitti, "Male and Female Brains Experience Humor Differently," FoxNews.com, November 9, 2005, accessed March 28, 2010, http://www.foxnews .com/story/0,2933,175092,00.html.

49. Naranjo-Huebl, "From Peek-a-boo to Sarcasm," p. 352.

50. Paul E. McGhee, "The Role of Laughter and Humor in Growing Up Female," in *Becoming Female: Perspectives on Development*, edited by Claire B. Kopp, in collaboration with Martha Kirkpatrick (New York: Springer, 1979), pp. 186–99.

51. Ibid., p. 309.

52. Ibid., pp. 125–26, 131.

53. Ibid., p. 289.

54. *Double-Bind Dilemma for Women in Leadership*, p. 27.

55. Ibid.

56. Kathleen Gerson, *The Unfinished Revolution: How a New Generation Is Reshaping Family, Work, and Gender in America* (Oxford: Oxford University Press, 2010).

57. Ibid., p. 3.

CHAPTER 3: Roar of the Crowd

1. Kathleen Hall Jamieson, *Beyond the Double Bind: Women and Leadership* (New York: Oxford University Press, 1995), p. 3.

2. Ibid.

3. Dee Dee Myers, *Why Women Should Rule the World* (New York: Harper-Collins Publishers, 2008), p. 41.

4. Anne E. Kornblut, *Notes from the Cracked Ceiling: Hillary Clinton, Sarah Palin, and What It Will Take for a Woman to Win* (New York: Crown Publishers, 2009), pp. 33–34.

5. Myers, *Why Women Should Rule the World*, p. 42.

6. Caroline Turner, "Hillary Clinton and the Double Bind: Hope for a More Bal-

anced Kind of Leadership," Athena Group, 2008, p. 2, accessed February 18, 2010, http://www.athenagroup.biz/whitepapers/whitepapers.html.

7. Kornblut, *Notes from the Cracked Ceiling*, pp. 35–36.

8. Turner, "Hillary Clinton and the Double Bind," p. 2.

9. Sylvia Ann Hewlett and Norma Vite-Leon, *High-Achieving Women, 2001* (New York: National Parenting Association, 2002), pp. 9–10.

10. Ibid., p. 10.

11. Ibid., p. 12.

12. Sylvia Ann Hewlett et al., *Sustaining High Performance in Difficult Times* (New York: Center for Work-Life Policy, 2008), p. 6.

13. National Institute of Child Health and Human Development, "Study of Early Child Care and Youth Development," accessed March 21, 2010, https://secc.rti.org/.

14. Liana C. Sayer, Suzanne M. Bianchi, and John P. Robinson, "Are Parents Investing Less in Children? Trends in Mothers' and Fathers' Time with Children," *American Journal of Sociology* 110, no. 1 (2004): 31–32.

15. Dan Antony, editorial, *University Register*, University of Minnesota (2004).

16. Thinkexist.com, accessed March 23, 2010, http://thinkexist.com/quotation/not_everything_that_is_faced_can_be_changed-but/7880.html.

CHAPTER 4: Bells and Whistles

1. Although technology is an equal-opportunity stressor (meaning, it's not specific to high-achieving women, as are many of the other stressors we've covered), the degree of accessibility it provides to high-achieving women is even more dangerous because rates of burnout are already so high.

2. Sylvia Ann Hewlett et al., *Seduction and Risk: The Emergence of Extreme Jobs* (New York: Center for Work-Life Policy, 2007), p. 18.

3. John Pilger, "Globalisation: New Rulers of the World," JohnPilger.com, accessed February 12, 2010, http://www.johnpilger.com/page.asp?partid=12.

4. Shamsi T. Iqbal and Eric Horvitz, "Disruption and Recovery of Computer Tasking: Field Study, Analysis, and Directions," *CHI* (2007): 677–86.

5. Ibid.

6. Ibid.

7. Gloria Mark, Daniela Gudith, and Ulrich Klocke, "The Cost of Interrupted Work: More Speed and Stress," *CHI* (2008): 107–110.

8. Linda Stone, "E-mail Apnea: A Diagnosis?" O'Reilly Radar, February 2008, accessed February 10, 2010, http://radar.oreilly.com/archives/2008/02/diagnosis-e-mail-apnea.html.

9. Mike Bloxham et al., "Video Consumer Mapping Study," Council for Research Excellence, March 26, 2009, accessed February 12, 2010, http://www.researchexcellence.com/vcmstudy.php.

10. Stone, "E-mail Apnea."

11. J. Miller McPherson, Linda Smith-Lovin, and Matthew E. Brashears, "Social Isolation in America: Changes in Core Discussion Networks over Two Decades," *American Sociological Review* 71, no. 3 (2006): 353–75.

12. Keith N. Hampton et al., "Social Isolation and New Technology: How the Internet and Mobile Devices Impact Americans' Social Networks," Pew Research Center, November 2009, accessed February 22, 2010, http://pewinternet.org/Reports/2009/18—Social-Isolation-and-New-Technology.aspx.

13. Linda Stone, "Beyond Simple Multi-Tasking: Continuous Partial Attention," Linda Stone Online, November 30, 2009, accessed February 10, 2010, http://lindastone.net/2009/11/30/beyond-simple-multi-tasking-continuous-partial-attention/.

14. Hewlett, *Seduction and Risk*, pp. 8–9.

15. Marcelle Pick, "Deep Breathing: The Truly Essential Exercise," *Women to Women*, February 16, 2010, accessed February 18, 2010, http://www.womentowomen.com/fatigueandstress/deepbreathing.aspx.

16. Farhad Manjoo, "An Empty In-Box, or with Just a Few E-mail Messages? Read On," *New York Times*, March 4, 2009, accessed March 18, 2010, http://www.nytimes.com/2009/03/05/technology/personaltech/05basics.html.

CHAPTER 5: Driving Too Fast for Conditions

1. Harriet Braiker, *The Type E* Woman: How to Overcome the Stress of Being Everything to Everybody* (Lincoln, NE: iUniverse, 2006), p. xi.

2. Steven Berglas, *Reclaiming the Fire: How Successful People Overcome Burnout* (New York: Random House, 2001), p. 21.

3. Linda Ellis Eastman, ed., *Overcoming the Superwoman Syndrome* (Prospect, KY: Professional Woman Publishing, 2007).

4. Allan Mallinger and Jeannette DeWyze, *Too Perfect: When Being in Control Gets Out of Control* (New York: Clarkson Potter, 1992); Alice Domar and Alice Lesch Kelly, *Be Happy without Being Perfect: How to Break Free from the Perfection Deception* (New York: Crown Publishers, 2008). Both of these books offer advice for overcoming perfectionism.

5. Braiker, *The Type E* Woman*, p. 224.

6. Gina Trapani, "How to Write To-Do Lists That Work," *Harvard Business Review*, January 13, 2009, accessed March 30, 2010, http://blogs.hbr.org/cs/2009/01/how_to_write_todo_lists_that_w.html.

7. Quote Garden, accessed March 24, 2010, http://www.quotegarden.com/laughter.html.

CHAPTER 6: Engine Check

1. Walter B. Cannon, *Bodily Changes in Pain, Hunger, Fear, and Rage: An Account of Recent Researches into the Function of Emotional Excitement* (New York: D. Appleton, 1915).

2. Hans Selye, *The Stress of Life* (New York: McGraw-Hill, 1978), pp. 29–79.

3. Shelley E. Taylor et al., "Biobehavioral Responses to Stress in Females: Tend-and-Befriend, Not Fight-or-Flight," *Psychological Review* 107, no. 3 (2000): 411–29; Shelley Taylor, "Tend and Befriend: Biobehavioral Bases of Affiliation under Stress," *Current Directions in Psychological Science* 15, no. 6 (2006): 273–77.

4. Dee Dee Myers, *Why Women Should Rule the World* (New York: Harper-Collins Publishers, 2008), p. 54.

5. *Stress in America*, American Psychological Association (Washington, DC: American Psychological Association, 2008), p. 8.

6. Kristin Francini and Lisa Tumminello, "Stressed Out Women Have No Time for Sleep," National Sleep Foundation, March 6, 2007, accessed March 18, 2010, http://www.sleepfoundation.org/article/sleep-america-polls/2007-women-and-sleep.

7. *Summary Findings of the 2007 Sleep in America Poll*, National Sleep Foundation (Washington, DC: National Sleep Foundation, 2007), p. 7.

8. *Stress in America*, p. 7.

9. John F. Rothrock, "The Truth about Triggers," *Headache* (2008): 499.

10. *Stress in America*, p. 8.

11. "What I Need to Know about Irritable Bowel Syndrome," National Digestive Diseases Information Clearinghouse, US Department of Health and Human Resources, National Institutes of Health, accessed March 21, 2010, http://digestive.niddk.nih.gov/ddiseases/pubs/ibs_ez/#stress; "Ulcerative Colitis," National Digestive Diseases Information Clearinghouse, US Department of Health and Human Resources, National Institutes of Health, February 2006, NIH Publication #06-1597, p. 2.

12. Sarah Berga, Tammy L. Daniels, and Donna E. Giles, "Women with Functional Hypothalamic Amenorrhea but Not Other Forms of Anovulation Display Amplified Cortisol Concentrations," *Fertility and Sterility* 67, no. 6 (1997): 1024–30; Benedetta Brundu et al., "Increased Cortisol in the Cerebrospinal Fluid of Women with Functional Hypothalmic Amenorrhea," *Journal of Clinical Endocrinology and Metabolism* 91, no. 4 (2006): 1561–65.

13. Dr. Sarah Berga, e-mail message to author, March 23, 2010.

14. Ibid.

15. "Stress Hormone, Depression Trigger Obesity in Girls," College of Health and Human Development, Pennsylvania State University, February 22, 2010, accessed February 25, 2010, http://www.hhdev.psu.edu/news/2010/2_22_10_obesity_study.html.

16. Dr. Jacalyn J. Robert-McComb, telephone interview with author, March 23, 2010. Dr. Robert-McComb is the coeditor and contributing author of the book *Eating Disorders in Women and Children: Prevention, Stress Management, and Treatment*, published by CRC Press in 2000.

17. Karen Asp, "Superwoman Syndrome Fuels Pill-Popping," MSNBC.com, February 24, 2010, accessed March 18, 2010, http://www.msnbc.msn.com/id/35526012/ns/health-behavior/.

18. Carolyn M. Mazure, Gwendolyn P. Keita, and Mary C. Blehar, *Summit on Women and Depression: Proceedings and Recommendations* (Washington, DC: American Psychological Association, 2002), p. 10.

19. Ibid., p. 15.

20. *Stress in America*, p. 7.

CHAPTER 7: Running on Empty

1. Debbie Mandel, *Addicted to Stress: A Woman's 7-Step Program to Reclaim Joy and Spontaneity in Life* (San Francisco: Jossey-Bass, 2008), p. 4.

2. Ahnna Lake, "Professional Burnout: Do You Have It?" *Vermont Bar Journal* 21, no. 1 (1995): 35–36.

CHAPTER 8: Refueling

1. Kristin Francini and Lisa Tumminello, "Stressed Out Women Have No Time for Sleep," National Sleep Foundation, March 6, 2007, accessed March 18, 2010, http://www.sleepfoundation.org/article/sleep-america-polls/2007-women-and-sleep.

2. "Sleep Deprivation Effects: An Overview," Sleep Deprivation Effects Online, accessed March 30, 2010, http://www.sleepdeprivationeffects.net/.

3. Patrick M. Fuller, Joshua J. Gooley, and Clifford B. Saper, "Neurobiology of the Sleep-Wake Cycle: Sleep Architecture, Circadian Regulation, and Regulatory Feedback, *Journal of Biological Rhythms* 21, no. 6 (2006): 482–93.

4. "Myth—and Facts—About Sleep," National Sleep Foundation, accessed March 26, 2010, http://www.sleepfoundation.org/article/how-sleep-works/myths-and-facts-about-sleep.

5. "What Happens When You Sleep," National Sleep Foundation, accessed March 26, 2010, http://www.sleepfoundation.org/article/how-sleep-works/what-happens-when-you-sleep.

6. Ibid.

7. "How Much Sleep Do We Really Need?" National Sleep Foundation, accessed March 26, 2010, http://www.sleepfoundation.org/article/how-sleep-works/how-much-sleep-do-we-really-need.

8. Ibid.

9. Barry M. Popkin, "The U.S. Diet and the Role of Beverages," 2006, accessed March 23, 2010, http://www.cpc.unc.edu/projects/beverage/publications.

10. "How Sweet Is It?" Nutrition Source, Harvard School of Public Health, accessed March 24, 2010, http://www.hsph.harvard.edu/nutritionsource/healthy-drinks/how-sweet-is-it/index.html.

11. "Choosing Healthy Drinks: The Bottom Line," Nutrition Source, Harvard School of Public Health, accessed March 24, 2010, http://www.hsph.harvard.edu/nutritionsource/healthy-drinks/.

12. Barry M. Popkin et al., "A New Proposed Guidance System for Beverage Consumption in the United States," *American Journal of Clinical Nutrition* 83, no. 3 (March 2006): 529–42; "Beverage Intake in the United States: Beverage Panel Recommendations and Analysis," University of North Carolina, accessed March 24, 2010, http://www.cpc.unc.edu/projects/beverage/panel_recommendations.

13. "How Much Physical Activity Do Adults Need?" Centers for Disease Control and Prevention, accessed March 24, 2010, http://www.cdc.gov/physicalactivity/everyone/guidelines/adults.html.

14. "Laughter Is Good for Your Heart," University of Maryland Medical Center, November 15, 2000, accessed March 24, 2010, http://www.umm.edu/news/releases/laughter.htm.

15. Jonathon R. B. Halbesleben and Denise M. Rotondo, "Developing Social Support in Employees: Human Resource Development Lessons from Same-Career Couples," *Advances in Developing Human Resources* 9 (2007): 544–55.

16. Ibid., pp. 548–49.

17. "Choose Your Extreme Adventure," Extreme Adventures, Abercrombie & Kent Online, accessed March 24, 2010, http://www.akextremeadventures.com/.

18. Although this quotation is often attributed to former senator Paul Tsongas, it appears that the credit actually goes to a Massachusetts attorney and friend of Paul Tsongas, Arnold Zack. See Ralph Keyes, *The Quote Verifier: Who Said What, Where, and When* (New York: St. Martin's Press, 2006), p. 42.

19. "Top 10 Extreme Vacations," ShermansTravel.com, accessed March 24, 2010, http://www.akextremeadventures.com/.

20. Sylvia Ann Hewlett et al., *Seduction and Risk: The Emergence of Extreme Jobs* (New York: Center for Work-Life Policy, 2007), p. 8.

21. Elizabeth Scott, "Life Meaning: Supporting a Worthy Cause Can Help Give Life Meaning," About.com: Stress Management, December 20, 2006, accessed March 24, 2010, http://stress.about.com/od/optimismspirituality/a/meaning.htm.

CHAPTER 9: Getting Back in the Driver's Seat

1. Commission on Lawyer Assistance Programs, American Bar Association. For more information, see http://www.abanet.org/legalservices/colap (accessed March 18, 2010).

2. Michael Beitler, "A Practitioner's Guide for Change Leaders and Consultants," 2005, accessed March 25, 2010, http://www.mikebeitler.com/freestuff/Overcoming-Resistance-to-Change.pdf; Elkind Group, accessed March 25, 2010, http://elkindgroup.com/products/overview.asp.

3. "Empowering Quotes," BeingLive.com, accessed March 24, 2010, http://www.beinglive.com/Empowering-Quotes.aspx.

EPILOGUE

1. Christina Maslach and Michael P. Leiter, *The Truth about Burnout: How Organizations Cause Personal Stress and What to Do about It* (San Francisco: Jossey-Bass, 1997), p. 18.

2. Ibid., p. 34.

3. Ibid., p. 148.

4. "Top Companies Show Investing in Employee Health and Well-Being Leads to Business Success," American Psychological Association, March 5, 2007, accessed March 25, 2010, http://www.apa.org/news/press/releases/2007/03/phwa.aspx.

5. Stephen Walker, "What Every CEO-COO Should Know about the Costs of a Heart Attack or Stroke," March 10, 2010, accessed March 25, 2010, http://www.drstephenwalker.com/2010/03/10/what-every-ceo-coo-should-know-about-the-cost-of-a-heart-attack-or-stroke/.

6. Maslach and Leiter, *Truth about Burnout*, p. 75.

7. Ibid., pp. 103–104.

8. Steven Berglas, *Reclaiming the Fire: How Successful People Overcome Burnout* (New York: Random House, 2001), pp. 186–88.

9. Ibid., p. 188.

10. Ibid., pp. 188–89.

11. Jennifer Ludden, "When Employers Make Room for Work-Life Balance," NPR, March 15, 2010, accessed March 25, 2010, http://www.npr.org/templates/story/story.php?storyId=124611210.

12. Office of the Press Secretary, White House, March 23, 2010, accessed March 26, 2010, http://www.whitehouse.gov/the-press-office/white-house-announces-forum-workplace-flexibility.

13. Kerry Panchuk, "Is the Virtual Office the Future? Regus Report Suggests So," *Dallas Business Journal*, March 16, 2010, accessed March 26, 2010, http://dallas.bizjournals.com/dallas/stories/2010/03/15/daily12.html.

14. Sylvia Ann Hewlett et al., *Seduction and Risk: The Emergence of Extreme Jobs* (New York: Center for Work-Life Policy, 2007), p. 37.

15. Sandy Burud, "Mastering the Art of a Flexible Culture: How the *Working Mother* 100 Best Companies Create a Flexible Culture," October 2009, accessed March 26, 2010, http://wfnetwork.bc.edu/blog/predictions-for-2010-about-workplace-flexibility.

16. "Working Mother 100 Best Companies 2009," Working Mother, accessed March 26, 2010, http://www.workingmother.com/BestCompanies/work-life-balance/2009/08/working-mother-100-best-companies-2009.

17. "100 Best Companies to Work For," Fortune, CNNMoney.com, accessed March 26, 2010, http://money.cnn.com/magazines/fortune/bestcompanies/2010/snapshots/1.html.

18. Steven Rosenberg, "Perks, Job Security Make Firm 'Best U.S. Employer,'" Boston.com, accessed March 26, 2010, http://www.boston.com/news/local/articles/2010/03/14/software_firm_with_middleton_branch_wins_best_us_employer_title/.

19. "Work/Life Benefits," Abbott Laboratories, accessed March 18, 2010, http://www.abbott.com/global/url/content/en_US/40.65.25:25/general_content/General_Content_00286.htm.

20. Burud, "Mastering the Art of a Flexible Culture."

21. Hewlett, *Seduction and Risk*, p. 39.

22. Emma Donaldson-Feilder, Rachel Lewis, and Joanna Yarker, "Preventing Stress: Promoting Positive Manager Behaviour: CIPD Insight Report," CIPD, 2009, accessed March 30, 2010, http://www.cipd.co.uk/subjects/health/stress/_preventing_stress.

23. Marlene Kramer, *Reality Shock: Why Nurses Leave Nursing* (St. Louis: CV Mosby, 1974).

24. Brad Harrington and Jamie J. Ladge, "Got Talent? It Isn't Hard to Find: Rec-

ognizing and Rewarding the Value Women Create in the Workplace," Shriver Report, accessed March 25, 2010, http://www.awomansnation.com/business.php.

25. Marti Barletta, *Marketing to Women: How to Understand, Reach, and Increase Your Share of the World's Largest Market Segment* (Chicago: Dearborn Trade Publishing, 2003), p. 3.

26. Lois Joy et al., "The Bottom Line: Corporate Performance and Women's Representation on Boards," accessed March 24, 2010, http://www.catalyst.org /publication/200/the-bottom-line-corporate-performance-and-womens-representation -on-boards.

27. Georges Desvaux, Sandrine Devilliard-Hoellinger, and Mary C. Meaney, "A Business Case for Women," *McKinsey Quarterly*, September 2008, accessed February 23, 2010, https://www.mckinseyquarterly.com/A_business_case_for_women_ 2192.

28. Rebecca Tuhus-Dubrow, "The Female Advantage: A New Reason for Businesses to Promote Women: It's More Profitable," *Boston Globe*, March 3, 2009, accessed March 18, 2010, http://www.boston.com/bostonglobe/ideas/articles/2009/ 05/03/the_female _advantage/.

29. Michele L. Swers, *The Difference Women Make: The Policy Impact of Women in Congress* (Chicago: University of Chicago Press, 2002), pp. 97–110.

30. Rosenberg, "Perks, Job Security Make Firm 'Best U.S. Employer.'"

31. Kathleen Gerson, *The Unfinished Revolution: How a New Generation Is Reshaping Family, Work, and Gender in America* (Oxford: Oxford University Press, 2010), p. 3.

32. Ibid., p. 104.

33. "Amelia Earhart," Word Press, accessed March 24, 2010, http://quotes.word press.com/ 2006/06/25/amelia-earhart/.

INDEX